Praise for
Lessons Learned

Roland Barth's warm and wise book deserves to be kept close at hand, maybe with a sign saying, "Open in case of emergency!" Whenever work takes one of its distressing or depressing turns, just scan the table of contents for the chapter that fits. Barth has mined his own experiences for a wonderful collection of tales that use open-water sailing as a powerful metaphor for work and life. By turns witty, entertaining, instructive and poignant, Barth's stories will get you thinking. The "working rules" salted throughout the book will help you navigate the deceptive shoals and powerful tides we all have to deal with at work.

—Lee G. Bolman
Marion Bloch/Missouri Chair in Leadership
Bloch School of Business and Public Administration
University of Missouri - Kansas City
Coauthor, *Leading With Soul*

Roland Barth skillfully applies lessons learned from cruising on the Maine coast to both the personal and professional relationships on dry land. Barth writes with great humor and telling insight, drawing on his distinguished career as an educator and his avocation as a yachtsman. His Lessons Learned *apply to us all: truths which capture essential wisdom for both happiness and success at home and work.*

—Daniel S. Cheever, Jr.
President, Simmons College

Whether a sailor or a school administrator, on a boat or in a boardroom, at sea or ashore, Barth's "Lessons" are powerful guides for defining the types of interpersonal relationships needed to bring about success.

—Karen M. Dyer
Manager, Education Sector
Center for Creative Leadership
Coauthor, *The Intuitive Principal*

Roland Barth is a master storyteller. In this book, he draws from the experiences of his two passions, sailing and education, to bring important and useful lessons to his readers. This is an entertaining and fast read. Barth's lessons are worth learning.

—Vincent L. Ferrandino
Executive Director
National Association of Elementary School Principals

Roland Barth presents us with a delightful series of life's lessons equally applicable to the high seas and to the daily workplace of landlubbers. Twenty-four "Cruising Rules" matched with twenty-four "Working Rules" represent the distilled wisdom from a master who has spent forty years leading and learning his way through life to the benefit of others. An invaluable guide to personal and organizational effectiveness.

—Michael Fullan
Dean
Ontario Institute for Studies in Education
University of Toronto
Author, *The Moral Imperative of School Leadership*

More than any other writer on educational leadership of the past 25 years, Roland Barth has consistently engaged the emotional side of school life and its impact on school teachers, leaders, and their communities.

These stories entertain, inform, and stimulate reflection about relationships in the workplace. The working rules will no doubt find their way onto calendars, diaries and post-it notes as reminders for right living and working. In this era driven by educational research, standards and policies, thankfully, Roland Barth's voice continues to remind us of the importance of people, even as his wisdom points us gently in the direction of humane yet practical action.

—Philip Hallinger
Executive Director of Management
Mahidol University

Roland Barth leads us school practitioners to reflect upon our work by using the deceptively simple art of storytelling to share lessons learned. Barth reminds us that relationship building is still key to creating and sustaining high performing schools. In this way, he walks the reader through the many practical strategies educators can – and must – use to grapple with the continuous adaptive challenges inherent in learning communities.

—Linda Phillips Hollomon
Executive Director
Office of Professional Development
Atlanta Public Schools

With Lessons Learned, *Barth unites his passion for sailing with his love for schooling. The result is a new kind of wisdom, one born from the integration of experiences with and reflections about life in all of its manifestations. The wisdom pulls us back to think anew about relationships, forgiveness, and responsibilities.*

—Linda Lambert
Professor Emeritus, California State University, Hayward
Founding Director
Center for Educational Leadership
Author, *Building Leadership Capacity in Schools*

This book is for leaders, partners, followers, rookies, longtime pros, visionaries, and day-to-day people. Roland Barth's Lessons Learned *is a revelation about "school" and those who practice in it. To read it is to be inspired, heartened, startled, delighted. Barth talks to us with candor and humor and astuteness. He makes us suddenly say, "Yes, he's right – I wish I'd thought of that!" or, better, "That's what I always knew on my best days but too easily let it slip . . . !"*

Barth uses the metaphor of sailing with deceptive modesty and power. His meanings come to us often playfully, always with conviction. They stick in the mind and heart.

—David Mallery
Director of Professional Development
National Association of Independent Schools

What fun! I found myself wanting to steal all his quotes and rules, and fill them in with my own stories. He left me making New Year's resolutions and then laughing at myself. In short, he turned sailing and minding school into grand adventures, and led me inevitably to imagine what fun it would be to do both in his company. Roland Barth turns reflective craftsmanship into a revealing and wonderful venture, as he travels over and under troubled waters, and comes up each time with a new way to see an old dilemma.

—Deborah Meier
Co-Principal
Mission Hill School (Boston)
Author, *In Schools We Trust*

Lessons Learned *is an insightful, funny, moving look at commonalities between life at sea and life in the schoolhouse. Using his head and heart, Roland Barth applies the many lessons learned from sailing (Cruising Rules) to the work of school leadership (Working Rules). Combining the two makes for much shared wisdom and serious fun. More than any other Barth book, this one exposes Roland for what he really is, an avid sailor, loyal friend, life-long learner, and compassionate leader.*

—Millie Pierce
Director
The Principal's Center
Harvard Graduate School of Education
Coeditor, *The 21st-Century Principal*

If you're curious about how to strengthen and sustain relationships in life, you'll relish Lessons Learned. *If you are a school leader who wants to build strong organizational culture, you'll find it essential.*

—Jonathon Saphier
Founder and Chairman of the Board
Research for Better Teaching

Lessons Learned *is a charming, funny, and wise book that teaches important lessons about relationships at work and play. Once again Barth has written a useful book for teachers and principals alike.*

—Thomas J. Sergiovanni
Lilian Radford Professor of Education
Trinity University
Author, *Leadership for the Schoolhouse*

Other Titles by Roland S. Barth

Roland S. Barth

Lessons Learned

Shaping Relationships and the Culture of the Workplace

CORWIN PRESS, INC.
A Sage Publications Company
Thousand Oaks, California

For information:

Corwin Press, Inc.
A Sage Publications Company
2455 Teller Road
Thousand Oaks, California 91320
www.corwinpress.com

Sage Publications Ltd.
6 Bonhill Street
London EC2A 4PU
United Kingdom

Sage Publications India Pvt. Ltd.
B-42, Panchsheel Enclave
Post Box 4109
New Delhi 110 017 India

Printed in the United States of America

Library of Congress Cataloging-in-Publication Data

Barth, Roland S.
Lessons learned : shaping relationships and the culture of the workplace / Roland S. Barth.
p. cm.
Includes bibliographical references and index.
ISBN 0-7619-3842-7 (Cloth) — ISBN 0-7619-3843-5 (Paper)
1. Organizational behavior. 2. Psychology, Industrial. 3. Interpersonal relations. 4. Corporate culture. I. Title.
HD58.7.B3717 2003
650.1′3—dc21
2003004727

This book is printed on acid-free paper.

05   06   07   7   6   5   4   3

Acquisitions Editor:	Robert D. Clouse
Editorial Assistant:	Jingle Vea
Production Editor:	Julia Parnell
Copy Editor:	Elizabeth Budd
Typesetter:	C&M Digitals (P) Ltd.
Proofreader:	Kathleen Pearsall
Cover Designer:	Michael Dubowe

Contents

Preface

Very little in our lives is more important and more pervasive than our relationships with those we care about and with whom we work. And very little is more inscrutable and problematic. Relationships can be as taxing and toxic as they can be replenishing and fulfilling.

"When in doubt—tell the truth," Mark Twain advised. Well, everything you are about to read is true. It all actually happened—to the best of my recollection. Unfortunately, my recollection of life with others over these many years is a bit blurry. So this is probably not *just* as it was, but rather the way I *remember* it was—a kind of impressionistic painting. Allow me some poetic license in writing, and I shall allow you the same in reading.

The details don't really matter that much, anyway. What matters is that our experiences carry with them astonishing learning. These stories, aged in my soul's cask over the years, are idiosyncratic, perhaps even peculiar. Yet they express metaphors and teachings that are universal and lasting for me—and perhaps useful for you. They are offered in hope that each of us may find abundant and buoyant joy in our all-too-brief passages with one another.

Welcome aboard!

—Roland S. Barth
Tavernier, Florida
Winter 2003

Acknowledgments

I want to thank all of those who have suffered my company these many years aboard ship and ashore; many wonderful moments in wonderful relationships.

And I want to note the pivotal role that my editor, Robb Clouse, has played in this endeavor. He had a vision for this volume and convinced me that there *was* a book here—and that I might write it. Additionally, he has offered valuable assistance in its composition and editing.

Most important, I would like to acknowledge the heroic assistance—and companionship—in this effort provided by my wife Barbara Bauman. She has joined me in living some of these stories and has been integral to the many stages of construction of the others: conceptualizing, writing, editing, and editing some more. Working together has been a blessing, which has deeply enriched our relationship. Many moving lessons learned.

About the Author

Roland S. Barth is a consultant to schools, school systems, state departments of education, universities, foundations, and businesses in the United States and abroad.

After receiving his bachelor of arts degree from Princeton University and master's and doctoral degrees in education from Harvard University, he served as a public school teacher and principal for fifteen years in Massachusetts, Connecticut, and California.

Barth received a Guggenheim Fellowship in 1976 and joined the faculty at the Harvard Graduate School of Education for thirteen years. During that time, he was Director of the Study on the Harvard Graduate School of Education and Schools, Founding Director of the Principals' Center and of the International Network of Principals' Centers, and Senior Lecturer on education. He has been an Academic Visitor at Oxford University and a member of the National Commission on Excellence in Educational Administration.

He received an honorary Doctor of Humane Letters from Lewis and Clark College and is the recipient of the 2002 Alumni Award for Outstanding Contribution to Education from the Harvard Graduate School of Education. He serves as a trustee of Hurricane Island Outward Bound School, a member of the board of Micro-Society Inc., Chairman of the Board of the Principal Residency Network, and a member of the Board of Editorial Advisors of the *Phi Delta Kappan*.

Roland Barth is the author of many articles and of five books: *Learning by Heart* (2001), *Cruising Rules* (1998), *Improving Schools From Within* (1990), *Run School Run* (1980), and *Open Education and the American School* (1972). His particular fields of interest are school leadership, school improvement from within, and the personal and professional development of educators. Central to his thinking is the concept of the school as a community of learners and leaders.

The father of two accomplished daughters, Joanna and Carolyn, Barth is also an avid sailor in Maine and Florida salt waters and a dedicated farmer. He and his wife Barbara live in Maine, Florida, and Boston.

To the memory of my mother, Ramona Sawyer Barth—
My first relationship

Setting Sail

Over my entire adult life I have sailed and worked. One or the other. And never the twain have met. After all, have you ever seen a bumper sticker pronouncing, "I'd rather be working?" In fact I have found sailing—surrounding myself by that vast saltwater moat—the perfect antidote to work. Just enough going on aboard to demand full attention and to blot out the preoccupations of the workplace. But not so much as to further exhaust me emotionally. I have written about sailing and I have written about work, mostly the work of education. *Lessons Learned* might be seen as an unusual kind of autobiography, integrating for the first time these quintessential parts of my life.

Cruising on a sailboat, in the relentless company of others, all the while confined in a small space, is a worthy enough subject to consider. But I find that relationships at sea also offer a rich metaphor useful in other domains. Life is a cruise. For instance, as a school principal, every September I used to set out with 450 kids, twice as many parents, and 45 teachers aboard for a new school year, hoping that we'd all arrive in June safely back into port, with no lives lost, no major damage, and still on speaking terms.

Relationships at work are every bit as complex as those aboard a sailing vessel. Warts appear in our relationships in the workplace at least as frequently as at sea. And so do adverse gales, fogs, tides, currents, and rocks. And making midcourse corrections in our interpersonal behavior is no less critical in one realm than the other.

I call my lessons learned at sea "Cruising Rules." They lead each chapter and provide a springboard. The latter part of each chapter then considers lessons learned about relationships at work— "Working Rules." Together, they constitute, from my life, *Lessons Learned.*

*Cruise: Two or more days spent continuously on a boat that is
underway, with stops for the night.*

—John Rousmaniere
The Annapolis Book of Seamanship

"Roland, are we on Cruising Rules yet?" With these words,
Snyder always comes aboard. Snyder and I owned a succession of
three Friendship sloops—graceful, gaff-rigged, wooden, turn-of-the-
century Maine coastal fishing boats. Sometimes he and his family
sailed together, sometimes my family and I sailed. But once a year
Snyder and I sailed—just the two of us. We called our brisk
Columbus Day cruising weekend on the coast of Maine "the boys'
night on the town." During our three or four days together, things
were different.

For instance, our cuisine. For our first "night on the town,"
Snyder brought a five-pound brick of cheddar cheese, a case of ale,
and two packages of Oreos. I arrived with a large hunk of Swiss
cheese, some beer, and Twinkies. Balance and nutrition could be
attended to ashore.

And our conversation was different. Snyder and I revel in
organic gardening. The more manure to dilute Maine's rocks, the
better. When you put seeds in manure with a little soil and add water,
you grow zucchini. Big ones. Lots of them. So the noble zucchini
became another companion at mealtime and the centerpiece for
many conversations at sea. We once spent an entire evening relating
the concept of "friendship" to the ubiquitous zucchini. Consider the
endless possibilities: A friend is someone who, when offered a zucchini, will accept it. A friend is one who, when he has an excess of
zucchini, will not offer you any.

But mariners know that compatibility on board a sailing vessel
is a far more complex and fragile matter than zucchini. As our
annual adventures began to accumulate, Snyder and I found ourselves running up against the abundant and inevitable imperfections
of the other and even the occasional blemish in ourselves. Countless
hours living together in a confined, floating space, denied relief by a
cold, salty moat, makes things ripe for tension, even conflict.

The first night of one blustery, October cruise found us hunker-
ing down on an anchor in Muscongus Bay, as a gale-force wind
howled above. There we lay Friday night. And Saturday. And
Sunday. Plenty of time to get on each other's nerves. I believe it was

during these days of unrelenting intimacy that we promulgated and began to develop the art form that has come to be known as "Cruising Rules."

 Cruising Rules are the norms of personal behavior required for individuals to stay on speaking, even friendly, terms while confined together for an indefinite period in close quarters at sea.

Put bluntly, these Rules determine whether my sailing companions and I return to port cordially, angrily, separately, together—or not at all.

Over time the Rules have been employed, tested, and refined. The result, I am proud to say, is that my sailing companions and I continue to cruise happily together on sea and land alike.

Hard work spotlights the character of people: some turn up their sleeves, some turn up their noses, and some don't turn up at all.

—Sam Ewing

The literature on adult development tells us that as we enter our golden years we are beset with a deep desire to look back upon our lives, tease out what we have learned, and pass it on to the younger, upcoming generations. But learning from experience isn't inevitable. We must be intentional about it.

As a recovering academic, I am all too familiar with a critique of that culture once offered by Mortimer Adler: "The notes of the lecturer are passed to the notes of the listener—without going through the mind of either." I'm not sure how much wisdom or how much truth you will find in the pages to follow, but I can assure you *my* notes are different. They were accumulated not from libraries or from the academy, but from years in the workplace.

Some call it "reflection." Reflection is nothing less than an internal dialogue with oneself. It is the process of bringing past experiences to a conscious level, analyzing them, and determining better ways to think and behave in the future. Stepping back at the end of the day, month, year, or career and reflecting on success and failure and on one's part in both is a most worthwhile endeavor. And applying the lessons learned in new settings is even more worthwhile. And sometimes reflection invites us to share the fruits of this internal conversation with others. Such is my intent here.

I call what one acquires from experience on the job and from reflecting upon it "craft knowledge." It's what we learn in the school of hard knocks by showing up. It is my purpose to stow aboard this little volume as much of my craft knowledge as it will hold. Here you will find not only what I have learned about relationships at sea, but also what I have learned about relationships in forty heady, hearty years at work.

 ***Working Rules** are the norms of personal and professional behavior required for individuals in the workplace to stay on friendly terms and, in addition, to produce a distinguished product.*

Sailors are fond of the dictum "You cannot discover new oceans until you risk leaving sight of shore." I invite you now to join me as we go out of sight of familiar lands to explore relationships at sea and in the workplace.

Bon voyage!

CHAPTER 1

Have I Told You the One About . . . ?

During long periods becalmed, sailing a long tack, or at anchor over beer and cheese, some often tedious, though pragmatic, conversation takes place aboard. "Snyder, while you're below could you get . . .?" "Take the helm for a while, would you?" "What's the chart say about the depth off of Webber Dry Ledge?"

Occasionally, this discourse is elevated to the realm of "story." We are all, of course, packed to the gunwales with stories ready to be unloaded. One nineteenth-century rabbi observed, "God so loved stories that he invented man." So nothing deflates a relationship at sea as quickly as beginning a promising story, only to have one's companion mutter, "Oh Roland, you told that one on our 1974 cruise through Eggemoggin Reach."

Yet it demeans the storyteller to have to preface every tale with the preamble, "Snyder, have I told you the one about . . .?" It is, after all, stressful to the aging, overtaxed human mind to remember to whom you have told what and when. The solution to this recurring plight became **Cruising Rule 1:**

 Any story worth telling is worth telling often.

It reassures and warms the soul to be able to tell your companion any story from your lifelong repertoire at any time and have it received with enraptured enthusiasm, as if heard for the first time.

I have become fascinated by the power of storytelling as a form of personal and professional development. And as a form of interpersonal development.

Why tell stories? Why listen to stories? What story is worth telling? Who determines how worthy a story is? People tell stories about events that have left an impression on their lives. Listening to the same stories again and again, we gain insight into what colleagues and friends value and who they are. Stories are important to the teller, and so listening to them—even several times over—strengthens relationships. By listening, one places value on the experience of another.

Craft knowledge is the collection of wisdom and insights one accumulates by showing up on the job. If ways can be found to unlock, celebrate, and exchange craft knowledge, how much better each of us can perform our work. Storytelling is one way.

Unfortunately, when someone in the workplace begins to tell a story, all too often eyes glaze over. For it is believed that when you scratch a worker, out will come not craft knowledge, but a war story!

War stories are *descriptions* of practice. "Let me tell you about the time I tried to fire an employee." Craft knowledge is description of practice accompanied by *analysis* of practice. "Let me tell you about the time I tried to fire an employee. Here is what I learned. If I were to do it over again, here's how I would do it." Now we have transformed the war story into craft knowledge. Pure gold!

By honoring storytelling in the workplace, we can facilitate the revelation and exchange of craft knowledge. By telling their stories to colleagues, workers analyze them, clarify them and elevate their experiences to the realm of helpful respectability. There is important learning in every story. We are truly one another's best teachers—novices and veterans alike. Indeed, I am convinced that if all of us were to regularly disclose our stories to our colleagues—even a small fraction of what we have learned during our careers—our organizations would be transformed overnight.

Hence, **Working Rule 1:**

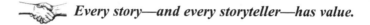 *Every story—and every storyteller—has value.*

Those who study it tell us that storytelling is a dying art form. After supper we used to gather around the kitchen table and tell our stories. Now we don't even eat together!

Part of the problem is that not all of us have "the narrative gene." Another part of the problem is that the culture of the workplace is not hospitable to our stories. And a large part is that we are not very good listeners. Jay O'Callahan, a New England storyteller, suggests that "A good listener is like a person with a thousand invisible hands, coaxing the story from the teller." To create a culture of storytelling, we need to create a culture of listening.

When we succeed in unlocking the power of storytelling in our organizations, we also deepen and strengthen the relationship between the tellers and the listeners. In some ancient cultures, everyone came to gatherings wearing a mask. But those who told stories were allowed to take off their masks. Indeed, telling and listening to stories can remove our feelings of distance, alienation, and invisibility from one another. We can bond as colleagues and learners. By telling and listening to one another's stories, we can make sense of the world of non-sense around us.

Chapter 2

The Long Version

Our lives are a trail of un-had conversations. One of the virtues of being at sea with a companion for an extended passage is the luxury of sufficient time for the "long version"—of everything. "Not that the story need be long, but it will take a long while to make it short" is the way sometime-mariner Henry David Thoreau put it. On a cruise it is possible to experience conversation with civility, grandeur, and complete resolution.

On the other hand, blessed with a captive audience, and the undisputed floor (or deck), nothing insults and assaults the speaker more than being unceremoniously interrupted while attempting the long version. Imagine a preacher delivering an arresting sermon from the pulpit only to have a member of the congregation butt in and interject a comment, question, or challenge! Hence, the necessity of **Cruising Rule 2:**

 When a party is talking, he is not to be interrupted until he has completed everything he wants to say.*

To be absolutely certain the speaker is indeed finished, a thirty-second interval should be observed at the conclusion of his words before another party commences speaking.

---

*The male pronoun is used throughout these sailing stories—advisedly.

Sailing vessels are stages for an extraordinary variety of performances: They are ego podiums. Nothing is so hospitable to a relationship at sea as having a fully attentive, respectful—and silent—audience.

So much information, so little time! On shore we must speak in code, abbreviation, and haste in the often-unsuccessful attempt to get our licks in before the next person intercedes or time expires. Indeed, this is precisely why many of us are forced to use the written word—so we can say *all of it* without interruption.

Speaking too much, too fast, clearly marks those who are land-locked in an office, in front of a class, or almost anywhere else. We rush through meetings, appointments, and phone calls so we can rush to the next meeting, appointment, or phone call. But we *can* slow down. We *must* slow down if we are to make our offices and homes habitable for human life.

And we must be respectful to each who would have his say. Have you ever made a presentation to a roomful of colleagues and noticed side conversations taking place around the room? I have. Or taught a class and had it disrupted by noisy students? I have. Been spoken over again and again in a social setting? I have. Had your boss's voice obliterate your own? I have!

If we hope to live our lives ashore "with civility, grandeur, and complete resolution," we must celebrate that same hope held by others. Although we may not be able to slip serenely off to sea, we can build stronger relationships by honoring what our peers and colleagues have to say. Hence, **Working Rule 2:**

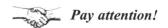 *Pay attention!*

There is much to learn by listening. After a colleague has spoken, engage in some active listening. Reflect back to the speaker, as honestly, fully, and "objectively" as you can, "here's what I hear you saying." Then—and only then—move to "here's what that says to me." Usually, of course, we jump right to "here's what that says to me," omitting the "here's what I hear you saying." The result: *no one* feels listened to. In a school, for instance, students don't feel listened to by teachers, teachers by administrators, and parents by anyone.

Learning is a social activity. We humans learn primarily from one another. Listening closely to what someone has to say reveals novel ideas that cement a friendship or grow a business. Listening builds confidence and trust—the cornerstones of every working relationship.

Chapter 3

Shootin' the Breeze

S ome stories aspire to the lofty status of humor—tales told for the fun of it and the fun in it. The medical profession has much to say about the benevolent qualities of humor. Western medical science has discovered that endorphins, pain-relieving chemicals produced by the brain, are released into the bloodstream when a person laughs. Clearly, laughter has an anesthetic property essential for good health—and for sustaining collective life in close quarters.

But one person's humor can be another's horror. What may be funny to me may be politically incorrect or not funny at all to you. Consequently, the telling of a story or a joke for the purpose of mirth places the narrator in a most vulnerable, even anxious position. When shooting the breeze, the mariner should allow the conversation, like the wind, to take him wherever it goes. Yet nothing so debilitates a relationship at sea as conveying what is an incontrovertibly funny story, only to be greeted by no response, by a critical response, or by a mere shake of the head. Hence **Cruising Rule 3:**

 A statement, joke, or story offered with the intent of humor shall be responded to with audible, visible, persistent, and, above all, authentic laughter.

So, when Snyder takes out his pipe, opens a beer, and clears his throat, it is time for rapt attention. When he begins to speak, and the first glimmer of a smile emerges from beneath his scruffy beard like a signal flag hoisted in the rigging, it is my cue to be ready. As his words roll into laughter, I respond with a timely signal flag of my own—an appropriate guffaw—as we enjoy a fleeting moment of camaraderie. The moment passes like ships at sea, and then we resume watch for the next sighting.

Who cares whether I hear it, get it, or like it!

Learning to laugh often and heartily is a fundamental survival strategy in the often-irrational world of work. Too often, the same decisions are made and actions taken that failed repeatedly in the past. Coworkers make statements so outrageous, so incomprehensible, you can't decide whether to cry, be angry, or simply shake your head in disbelief. In school settings, students repeat the same transgressions over and over again, leaving their teachers so bewildered that laughter may be the *only* recourse. In short, in the face of repetitive stupidity at work, we laugh or we go out of our minds.

Have you ever gotten anxious before a big presentation and found yourself giggling nervously? Laughter often brings relief. It permits us to cope. To stop taking the world so seriously, to be able to recognize that there are always life and death situations in the world infinitely more important than our day-to-day preoccupations, we must allow ourselves to laugh. The ability to find humor brings balance and humility to our lives even in the most trying and desperate times. It's especially calming to find humor in our own absurdity.

But do we need to laugh out loud? Certainly. If we want others to share in our mirth, and if we want to let others know we appreciate their jokes, their humanity, and their desire to find joy in life, we must make our own humor both visible and audible. What better way to build relationships than to share humor? When we know where a receptive, good-natured audience resides, we will seek that audience out and delight in it. Hence **Working Rule 3:**

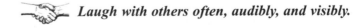 *Laugh with others often, audibly, and visibly.*

The average four-year-old laughs or smiles four hundred times each day; the typical adult laughs or smiles fifteen times each day. Clearly we have much to learn about playfulness from children, and from the child within us. No one wants to feel downtrodden or glum, and no one wants to be with those who are downtrodden or glum. Respond in kind to the good humor of others, and you'll lift your own mood and develop friendships that will endure over many years and careers. Laughter is the shortest distance between two people.

CHAPTER 4

The Fragile Ego

S ailors are a competent, authoritative lot whose knowledge base, particularly of sea lore and technical terms, far exceeds that of the powerboat crowd, let alone the landlubber. It should come as no surprise, then, that an impressed audience is essential to sustaining a relationship at sea. Nothing, on the other hand, is more corrosive than having one's wisdom questioned, challenged, or, heaven forbid, corrected. For example:

Roland: "Look at that beautiful Concordia yawl."

Snyder: "Roland, that's a Tahiti ketch."

This is an egregious affront not only to the fragile ego, but to a lasting friendship as well. Needed is acknowledgment of our unyielding desire to be right—and **Cruising Rule 4:**

 Any statement made as fact is, in fact, true and is therefore to be accepted as the truth.

Nothing bonds two sailors more than the appreciation by each of the wisdom of the other. So when Snyder studies the spar of a classy old sloop, anchored nearby, and pronounces, "Roland, hasn't she got a fine Park Avenue boom!" my only acceptable response is, "That sure is one fine Park Avenue boom!" Whatever the hell *that* is!

It is the human condition to speak with authority on matters about which we are not authorities. But how do we build and sustain lasting, trusting relationships with colleagues who—obvious to us, at least—pontificate, exaggerate, or stretch credulity? Surely each of us has worked with others who consistently chime in with "expert opinion" when it is apparent that they are not experts but merely proffering opinion. How to abide such gut-wrenching behavior?

All egos are fragile—male, female, subordinate, superordinate, beginner, and veteran alike. To deflate an inflated ego is a prickly, perilous pursuit. In the workplace, the most deflating pinprick occurs when we suggest that another may be . . . wrong! This can be, as they say, a CLM: a "career-limiting move."

Rather, in the workplace as well as at sea, best to adhere to **Working Rule 4:**

 Others know what they are talking about— unless proven otherwise.

It is by assuming coworkers' authority, authenticity and honesty that we honor and empower them. So begin with high expectations: People are what they say they are and seem to be. If they know not of what they speak, it will become apparent soon enough.

To let certain kinds of assertions pass without comment, however, may be irresponsible. If we are witnessing, for instance, not just an inflated ego but the dissemination of blatantly wrong information for which there will be costs, or if the imperious spoken words mask an unfounded, unwarranted attack on another, then we must intervene. Perhaps we confront a racist remark in a meeting. Perhaps independently we check data sources and provide correct information. Perhaps we confer with other colleagues about how best to respond.

It's a difficult balance: There are times in the workplace when each of us must not let stand unacceptable statements. At the same time, we must remember that each of us does not have to take on, single-handedly, the work of exposing the lie and revealing the truth.

No longer encumbered by fruitless efforts to challenge and correct the statements of others for their veracity, we'll find it less stressful to go to work and tolerate excessive pomp and questionable accuracy. Our role in life is not to lead a one-person "truth squad."

Our efforts are better directed at matters over which we have some control and influence, making damn sure what *we* say and what *we* do is considered and truthful. The best way we can contribute to a culture of integrity in the workplace is to speak and act with integrity ourselves. In the final analysis, as Mahatma Gandhi tells us, "We must *be* the change we wish to see in the world."

CHAPTER 5

Who Am I?

What we wear on the job, out to dinner, or at home often indicates how we want to be seen, or even who we want to become, as well as who we are. Over the years some remarkable costumes have come aboard. For instance, Gordon once rowed out in the dinghy wearing a three-piece suit, holding above his head a fancy silk parasol. Crissman once arrived in a navy blue double-breasted blazer with regimental striped tie, and a straw boater lashed down. Colorado cowboy Turnbull came aboard in a Stetson and boots. Thankfully, he left his spurs back at the 4-Bar Ranch.

And then there is Michael. This sartorial Iowan shows up for each cruise wearing a baseball cap with "Boar Semen" prominently emblazoned above the brim. Beneath is a week's stubble. Below that, he sports a chin-to-ankle fireman's coat seeking new life after weighty years of service on the back of a Baltimore city firefighter. Heavy metal clasps and fireproof fabric, in addition to virtually eliminating mobility, make it certain that, should this garment ever fall overboard (with or without its occupant), it will descend to Davy Jones's locker in record time! Emerging from beneath this peculiar foul-weather gear is a pair of 1940s seedy, red, high-topped sneakers rescued from Marty's cabin where they were found, on Marty—a few days after his death. "Michael's dead man's clothes," his wife calls them.

On my part, clothing is strictly practical. What I wear on the boat is at the bottom of a descending food chain of increasingly tattered apparel chronically recycled, but never quite discarded. I wear my "good" pants and shirts in polite society. When they become "tendah" (as they say Down East), they are remanded to the farm where they serve dedicated years shoveling manure, planting onions, and tinkering with tractors. When worn knees and elbows no longer offer protection from the marauding spring black flies, the clothes have exhausted their agrarian usefulness and are mercifully transported to sea, where there are no blackflies, to enjoy their last incarnation as "apparel." Thereafter, they assume a final lifetime as rags, useful for cleaning up after a mackerel catch. Thence, an honorable burial at sea.

On a passage, what we wear is also who we are—at the moment, that is. Fisherman, farmer, doctor, lawyer, fireman, chef, professor, athlete, yachtsman—and therein lies the rub. For all of the familiar, reassuring, and hallowed traditions of our nights on the town, Snyder and I frequently show up for a cruise with a new garment, awaiting sea trial. What we are doing, of course, is trying on a new "me." There is, needless to say, considerable vulnerability and risk attendant to trying on anything new, let alone a new persona.

After one excruciatingly long winter during which the need for boats was fulfilled by only an occasional perusal of marine mail-order catalogs, I arrived for a cruise with a new and, I thought, particularly "salty" sou'wester, the kind of headgear that only a real Newfoundlander or perhaps Gloucester hand-line fisherman might don. At the first hint of moisture in the air, I went below and emerged from the companionway thus attired, only to have Snyder greet me with, "Roland, where the hell did you get that ridiculous hat?" I suddenly came in touch with what some members of the male species have learned to call "a feeling," a hurt feeling. After determining there was no intent of humor and after discussing my wounds and identity crisis (the long version), we decided to institute **Cruising Rule 5:**

 Whoever you show up as for a cruise is who you are, and you are to be received accordingly.

So, when Snyder subsequently returned from a trip to Holland and, on the very first morning of a "boys' night on the town," self-consciously unveiled a new, black, shiny-visored Dutch sea captain's cap bordered in braid (rather pretentious, I thought), my immediate, mandatory, and only possible response could be, "Mornin', Captain—Sir!"

~~~~~~~~~

"Dress for success" is a familiar adage that plays out in every setting. I once met a fly fisherman wetting a line for the first time. He was attired in $300 waders, a fancy new L.L. Bean fishing vest, and sported a $2,000 G. Loomis fly rod. A total novice, he hoped that dressing the part—or what he thought the part required— would help him acquire the requisite skills that would surely follow with time and practice. And he was certain that the clothing and equipment would rub off on him some confidence helpful in gaining mastery of this exacting art form. Although he was violating Thoreau's advice—"Never engage in an enterprise which demands new clothing"—maybe he was right!

Each of us assumes many roles in life, frequently simultane-ously—husband, wife, father, mother, breadwinner, sailor, fly fisher-man. Yet for some reason we lock "the real me" in the car at the parking lot each morning and enter the workplace donning yet another role, one calculated for the occasion. Like the fly fisherman, we believe this persona will build confidence and lead to success.

My experience suggests that a rich and successful organizational culture is one into which members bring their real selves. It is a culture in which workers, to be sure, adopt behaviors necessary for teamwork, collegiality, productivity, and inventiveness. But a yeasty work culture is also one whose members retain their authenticity as parent, spouse, sailor, or fisherman. Such a culture encourages everyone to draw upon who they are and what they have learned in all of these other roles. To require a "dress code," to deny individu-als the right to be fully who they are, denies the organization the full measure of talent inherent in every one of us. How much we have learned about patience and finesse from fly fishing; how much we know about resourcefulness and adventure from sailing; how much we know about commitment and teamwork from the family. How desperately the workplace needs these qualities.

Accepting the persona that others assume fosters understanding and growth. Consequently, respecting this rich variety of roles is a "working rule" of major consequence. By inviting the "real me" to show up for work each day—by not permitting it to languish in the parking lot—we sustain, inform, and improve our work together.

Needed in large, printed letters is a sign visible as we leave the parking lot and enter the building that announces **Working Rule 5:**

 Bring your real self in, and accept and celebrate colleagues who bring their real selves in.

Many organizations designate a day each year to bring our sons and daughters to work. What if we designated every day as one to bring our *self* to work?

The colleague who wears his Dutch seaman's cap or African dashiki to work, or sports over her desk a trophy photo of "the big one that did not get away" or of family at a recent birthday party is to be honored. For this colleague has taken the risk of disclosing who he or she really is, and of discarding the protective layers so many wear to shield them from the slings and arrows of the workplace. These are the very layers that distance us from one another. An organization could do no better than to be replete with individuals.

CHAPTER 6

Steer Clear

I soon learned that not quite all shipboard conversation is to be allowed completion, is funny, is worth telling, or is true. I also found out that one cannot always be who he is.

East wind today. West wind coming up. A long-married couple and I decided upon a modest, three-day cruise from Muscongus Bay to Casco Bay, and back. Early in the cruise, I began to talk about a book I'd recently read on the topic of anger. Before we knew it, we were examining what causes each of us to become angry—and how we express it (or don't). And, before we knew it, we were angry discussing our anger! As more and more flotsam and jetsam from the past began to bob to the surface, storm warnings flew. Recognizing that this was only the morning of day one, with two more days together, we had no difficulty securing a majority vote to switch topics.

Politics. Bad choice. Republicans and Democrats on board soon became embroiled in corporate corruption, the environment, and taxes. Suddenly new fault lines emerged. Should chief executive officers be paid four hundred times as much as their employees? If taxes were reduced, just *who* would pocket the money? Does the American Civil Liberties Union really protect individual rights, or does it trample on the rights of the majority?

Three long-standing friendships began to unravel. Again. Somehow we had drifted back to anger, and it was still only day one. Days two and three were beginning to look bleak.

Then, suddenly, thankfully, out of the fray, like a welcome glow from Seguin Light, emerged **Cruising Rule 6:**

 Nondiscussibles may be discussed only within swimming distance of home port.

The implications are clear. Cruising people, upon coming aboard, must immediately take inventory of all potentially contentious and therefore hazardous cargo, such as politics, money, religion, family, feelings, sex, relationships . . . and anger.

All of these must be declared off limits and stowed. A vigilant watch must be maintained lest other controversial topics sneak in.

Once the juicy, volatile topics are edited from our time together, it may seem little is left to talk about. But as the three of us discovered, now peacefully sailing across the mouths of the Damariscotta, Sheepscot, and Kennebec rivers, a rather generous list of permissible and safe topics remains. Weather: wind, no wind; rain, no rain; fog, no fog. Food: what to eat, when to eat, where to eat, and who will prepare for and clean up after the eating. Landmarks: Christmas Cove or Damariscove; the Cuckolds or Ram Island? Seawater: how cold is it? Tide coming in or going out? How strong is the current? How steep are the waves? And other vessels: pretty, ugly, classy, tacky, "glass," wood? And, of course, lobster pot buoys: "God, there are a lot of them!"; colors, strategies for avoiding them, and their use as navigation aids.

The British were not the world's greatest sea power for nothing. They had it right: decorum, taste, and good breeding at all times, especially when facing imminent danger. Their success during naval battle can be attributed to their unyielding avoidance of interpersonal battle.

We discovered, on our little cruise, topics and conversations aboard a sailing ship that were safe, produced no anxiety, and caused no risk or damage to those on board. Limiting ourselves to these ensured the tranquil passage of many nautical miles—and days two and three. All other conversation had to wait until just moments before the cruise was over—when we could afford to live with the fallout.

W hen is one close enough to shore to discuss the non-discussibles, the sacred cows of the workplace? When is the right time to name and confront the rules, customs, and behaviors that permeate—and often debilitate—every organization?

Every work culture has commonly accepted practices, so familiar and often so politically charged, that taking them on seems to approach sacrilege—or suicide. "That's the way things are done around here."

Nondiscussibles are practices sufficiently important that they get talked about frequently. But they are so laden with taboos and fearfulness that these conversations take place only in the restrooms, at the water fountain, during the carpool home, or at the dinner table. They are indeed the elephants in the living room. Some small examples: named parking spaces for top executives, public transportation for the rest; stock options for some, but not for others; rigorous attention to the day's beginning and ending times for some, while others come and go as they please. Some larger examples: race, the underperforming colleague, leadership.

I believe the health of an organization is inversely proportional to the number of its nondiscussibles: the fewer the nondiscussibles, the healthier the culture; the more the nondiscussibles, the sicker it is.

Bound up in close quarters at sea, in order to preserve friend-ships—and return safely to port—it may make sense to leave non-discussibles alone. But what is one to do in the office? Unfortunately, it is impossible to much improve or strengthen a work culture while at the same time continuing to hold the nondiscussibles sacrosanct.

The workplace is a setting in which everyone has an obligation to contribute to the creation of a culture of productivity, continuous examination, experimentation, and improvement. In such a setting we can ill afford to give nondiscussibles power over us. Our professions are driven by progress—improving the quality of education, improving shareholder returns, improving the product.

In such goal-driven environments, everyone has a responsibility to examine and question norms and practices—and to encourage and welcome others who do the same. We must *not* "steer clear."

And we must not steer clear of **Working Rule 6:**

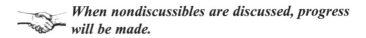 ***When nondiscussibles are discussed, progress will be made.***

But, of course, to challenge accepted practices and rules, to confront nondiscussibles, is often tantamount to challenging authority and those *in* authority. This is, of course, risky. But risk-free change is oxymoronic. The question is not whether to risk, but *how* to risk so that one's purposes are accomplished—without loss of life, limb, or career.

Here, prudent judgment must enter. When, where, and with whom you discuss nondiscussibles must be carefully considered. If addressing nondiscussibles is rooted in a desire for betterment of the organization, its employees, and its constituents (as well as one's own betterment), the risk taker moves to a higher ground. A greater degree of moral authority provides a greater safety strap. And taking risks in consultation and with the support of others, rather than going it alone, provides a second safety strap.

Always keep in mind what an old ballplayer Fred Wilcos once said: "Progress always involves risk. You can't steal second base and keep your foot on first."

CHAPTER 7

The Hand That Holds the Paintbrush

To purchase our first Friendship sloop, Snyder and I put together a syndicate of five owners, who each put up $500 for *Amos Swann.* She was a 26-foot, homely, leaky, and lovable little craft. With her came corroded fastenings, rotten garboards, and two well-worn pumps. And a 1924 Palmer make-or-break engine which required ten minutes to prime, choke, kick the flywheel (with an old rubber boot carried for the occasion), and, if you were lucky, start.

Our plan was to minimize not only our capital outlay but our maintenance expenses as well. So all of us agreed to assemble at the boatyard each spring to scrape, sand, and paint. Invitations were sent out and commitments secured. When the appointed May weekend arrived—cold, raw, and spitting snow—only two of us arrived with it. So, Snyder and I scraped and sanded. Sunday morning, with *Amos* all primed and ready to paint, we faced a crucial decision: What color should the house roof be? The arguments were between a clean white, an off-white, battleship gray, and what Snyder, for some mysterious reason, called "cat's-ass brindle." The latter—a brownish, orangeish, somewhat pukish buff, allegedly the authentic hue of the original Friendship sloop—probably evolved as a camouflage for fish entrails, lobster bait, and seaweed. We selected and applied, of course, the brindle.

The two of us, having diligently dispatched our boatyard duties for the fitting-out season, drove home with a feeling of considerable satisfaction, even virtue. This warm aura persisted until, one by one, the other three owners weighed in with their outrage over the dubious aesthetic properties of cat's-ass brindle as the proper topping for *their* boat.

A new rule emerged in time to save the day, the partnership, and the cat's-ass brindle. **Cruising Rule 7:**

 The hand that holds the paintbrush determines the color.

The following year we decided to pay the boatyard to scrape, sand, and paint.

A few years back, I was heading for an early morning faculty meeting. Our plan was to discuss an upcoming summer workshop and to assign and distribute among us the various tasks and responsibilities attendant to that workshop.

Driving in that morning, I got stuck in traffic. A truck had jack-knifed far ahead of me, and though the highway patrol was working hard to keep traffic going, it was barely moving. I missed the entire meeting.

When I finally arrived at school, I sought out the facilitator to see how things had gone without me.

"Fine," she said. "The meeting moved right along, and we were able to assign all of the tasks with no debate and very little discussion."

"Wonderful," I said. "What was I assigned?"

"Everything," she said with a smile. "We volunteered you for all of the arrangements, including booking the accommodations for the participants."

My initial reaction was protest. "The traffic . . . there was an accident . . . stop-and-go. . . ." I caught myself, however, realizing that my colleagues were having some fun at my expense. They had indeed assigned all the tasks to me. But in the end they were more than willing to share equitably the responsibilities.

The lesson they taught me, though, was crystal clear—**Working Rule 7:**

> *If you want to have your say, you've got to be present for the conversation.*

Good working relationships are built upon trust—that you'll be on time, that you'll not leave others to carry the workload in your absence, that you'll do what you say you will. People rely on your promises; they make plans around them. When you fail to follow through, you open the door and resentment steps in.

In a robust culture, you'll have colleagues like mine, who send a not-so-subtle message out of playfulness rather than resentment. Certainly they understand, as we all should, that circumstances can sometimes intervene. Fortunately, I was able to draw upon the capital of good relationships I had developed with them over the years.

But let us not forget, at work there is no boatyard to call upon to do it. We *all* must hold the paintbrush.

CHAPTER 8

Strength or Weakness?

The spring after *Amos Swann* finished dead last of fifty-four boats in the sloop races in Friendship—and nearly sank crossing the finish line—we sailed our second Friendship sloop down to Maine. Purchased in Massachusetts by a reconstructed consortium, *Moses Swann* was related to *Amos* in name only, neither to be confused with the Swan Boats of the Boston Public Garden. *Moses,* duly named and christened by my father (something of an Old Testament prophet himself), was younger, larger, and faster than *Amos*—despite an ugly propeller that extruded from the port buttock at a decidedly awkward angle. The other end of the shaft was attached to a rusty and unreliable gasoline engine, installed well after she was constructed in 1914.

It had been a beautiful sail from Swampscott—another leg of *Moses Swann*'s maiden voyage. A fresh sou'westerly had deposited us at the mouth of the York River, well into Maine waters. As the sun set, Donald, a new owner and expert sailor, and I furled the ample mainsail. We learned from a passing lobsterman that the village of York Harbor was upstream a mile or two. We motored against the ebbing tide, hailed a local fisherman, and inquired about a heavy mooring for the night in the swift river. He pointed out a vacant buoy in the lee of Stage Neck and assured us it was attached to two thousand pounds of granite. We led the hefty nylon pennant up over the chock, halfway out the bowsprit, and to the bitt on the foredeck. Thus secured, we went below to prepare and enjoy a serious zucchini-and-cheese casserole. After congratulating ourselves on the day's passage, we fell asleep, comforted by a gentle breeze and the secure mooring.

Sometime in the middle of the very dark night, we were abruptly roused by an ominous jolt. Leaping to our bare feet, and after depositing generous pieces of scalp on the cabin timbers overhead, we peered out the starboard portholes. To our dismay, we beheld a very large, very fancy motoryacht pummeling our defenseless vessel as a good breeze began to build. Full of indignant anger, we shot up the companionway to hail its sleeping and derelict crew. We immediately fell flat onto the deck, which was sloping forward at a cataclysmic angle. We crept cautiously and uncomprehendingly down the incline to discover, to our horror, that the entire bowsprit—and a good section of the bow—were below water. Turning aft, the stern confronted us like the tail of a bottom-feeding duck.

With all the perspicacity and analytical skills that only two groggy, off-duty professors could summon, we surmised that it was *we* who were adrift, now passing the first yacht and about to collide with a second—still secured to our reliable mooring. We deduced that *Moses Swann,* in the lunar tide, had lifted the mooring off of its familiar home in the mud and was now attempting to transport this pendulum to a new location across York Harbor. The pennant had been too short to extend from the mooring over the bowsprit to the samson post on deck. The tide had been too high. And we had been too innocent to foresee this physical impossibility.

Then we heard the water—seawater—trickling through the ill-fitting forward hatch and anchor hawsepipe. Were we sinking? What to do? Two thousand pounds of strain made it impossible to release the mooring, and a knife to the pennant would make some York Harbor fisherman very unhappy.

In the pitch darkness, we donned life jackets and prepared our dinghy (now lifeboat) with essentials—a gallon of fresh water and two wallets. Deciding that shallow water was preferable to deep if *Moses Swann* was going down, we turned to the engine—which, uncharacteristically, started like a thoroughbred—only to discover the propeller singing merrily in the air in the otherwise silent night. This was a situation for which our beginning Power Squadron course had left us unprepared. Maybe the advanced course?

Fortunately, the tide swept us toward yet another yacht tied up for the night against the wharf. Jumping aboard her, we managed, by flashlight, to secure *Moses* alongside and step off.

We pumped and maintained a "watch" (the meaning of which has never been clearer) for the rest of the night. By morning the tide was out, the mooring stone was becoming accustomed to its new latitude and longitude, and the bow had reemerged from the brine.

We had plenty of time during those wee hours to ponder the meaning of it all. Initial thoughts were of liability. Who was "at fault" here? Certainly not the yacht we collided with, which awakened us; nor *Moses* who delivered us safely; nor the fisherman who offered the mooring; nor the weighty stone, which could have been weightier. Finally, after holding a brief faculty meeting, it was decided that this unfortunate incident could not have been *our* fault.

Upon deeper reflection, **Cruising Rule 8** was born that dark night in York Harbor, Maine, amidst the mud, granite, nylon, wood, and water:

 That which secures us may also sink us.

The meeting was adjourned with the resolution that we had just experienced what marine insurance policies refer to as "an Act of God."

A ll of us work hard in this life. We invest considerable time, energy and usually money in acquiring and strengthening skills and knowledge that will contribute to our success. When we are successful, even if only moderately, we are likely to look back proudly on our efforts and then work even harder.

And perhaps we have certain personal characteristics—say, a great sense of humor or a tremendous sense of compassion for the less fortunate—that serve us well and cause others to admire us, to want to be like us.

Then, just when we thought everything was all set, the world changes. We take a new job. We move to a new community. We get married. Our children become teenagers. And suddenly, we're not as comfortable as we were—and perhaps not as successful. The jokes that had our elementary school children rolling on the floor now cause the teenagers to roll their eyes. The skill and efficiency with which we moved a project to completion in a former job is perceived as "steamrolling" over the staff in a new setting. Hey! What happened here?

As Gloria Swanson, playing the faded star of silent films, said in the movie *Hollywood Boulevard:* "I'm still big; it's the pictures that got small!"

Thus, **Working Rule 8:**

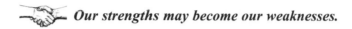 *Our strengths may become our weaknesses.*

It's painful, but essential, to realize that a cherished asset—a personality trait, a well-ingrained work habit—has become a liability. But the consequences of failing to do so can be devastating.

I know of a university professor who over the years developed a very successful working relationship with the publisher of his many books. Being entrepreneurial, he decided to leave his secure post as a tenured faculty member to accept a position on the publisher's editorial board. Here again he became quite established and secure.

Then, a larger company acquired the publishing house, and a new management team was installed. The professor had to part with his long-time colleague, the publisher. As the new management team introduced its models and ideas, the professor reminded them that he had learned the business a different way, and to great success, including consistent growth in revenue and profits. When matters became contentious, he even invoked the name of his friend, the former publisher. The new publisher, doubting the professor's loyalty and wanting to create a culture of support and fresh thinking, fired him.

When our assets become our liabilities, we are faced with two options: change ourselves or change the environment around us.

That which secures us may also sink us—indeed!

CHAPTER 9

Good Though

Next to sinking, nothing can make or break a cruise like eating. Food. Planning, anticipating, and savoring the next meal usually commences before the consumption of the current one. Sometimes there is a cook on board, occasionally a chef. But on most cruises, especially among men, there is a dramatically unfavorable ratio between the eager producers and eager consumers of fine meals.

Aboard ship, all of this is complicated by the unavailability of additional staples. The givens in the ship's locker lead to some rather peculiar meals late in a cruise—like mustard and cheese on moldy bread.

Donald, although a distinguished academic and superb sailor, experiences difficulty boiling a zucchini. As we were leaving York Harbor, he prepared a rather unusual luncheon that met with my thinly disguised disapproval, whereupon he told me a timely story about two bachelors who enjoyed fine cuisine. Unfortunately, neither had much skill in preparing it.

Constant complaining about one another's cooking had placed their relationship at risk. In desperation, they devised a rule: "Whoever complains about a meal prepared by the other shall cook all meals for a week." One of the pair, wanting to be relinquished from cooking duties, devised an ingenious plot. He stopped in the park on the way home and scooped up off the curb some recent dog droppings. When he got home, it being *his* turn to cook, he prepared a fine soufflé which included this unusual ingredient, hoping the response from his roommate would yield many cooking-free days.

The roommate, upon taking a large bite, turned his face down and his nose up and with both accuracy and tact uttered, "This soufflé tastes like s—! Good though!"

This story led inexorably to **Cruising Rule 9:**

> *Whatever is cooked by someone else is to be received, savored, and celebrated with the words "Good though!"*

These days on our cruises, scrumptious cuisine emerges from the galley that includes zucchini á la veal Oscar—without the veal and Oscar. And steamy cheese tortellini—without the tortellini. And lobster thermidor—without the lobster. Followed by a liberal dash of frosty Ben & Jerry's Oreo Cookie ice cream—without the ice cream. All prepared and consumed with impunity and immunity. "Good though!"

~~~~~~~

Over the years, I have written about schools as communities of learners. The purpose of schools is, after all, to promote profound levels of human learning. A community of learners is an environment in which everyone is continuously engaged in the most important enterprise of the schoolhouse. Students, teachers, administrators, and parents alike—learning.

Evaluation and especially self-evaluation are highly and positively related to learning. Evaluation is no less important than encouragement. Feedback, including negative feedback, is essential for human growth. We all need evaluation on a regular basis—consultants and authors and sailors included!

Yet in my years working in many schools as a teacher and principal I have found nothing more toxic to attaining a healthy learning environment than an overdose of constant criticism. We can continue to give our best efforts only so long, in the face of the message, "this tastes like s—."

In one school where I was principal, the parents, a very well-educated and entitled bunch, held high, exacting (and different!)

expectations for the instruction their children received. They were especially adept at calling attention to teachers' behavior which they found objectionable. Little else was immune from their criticism either—the curriculum, the schedule, grouping practices, the cleanliness of the restrooms . . . and the leadership of the principal. It seemed that to get what they wanted, they started at the top—and worked up. One irate parent was moved to send a letter to President Nixon (with a copy to the superintendent) condemning my leadership. These parents I once characterized in a fit of exasperation as "severely gifted."

Of course there is much to find fault with in schools and other organizations. But faultfinding as a steady diet can be hazardous to a culture's health—as well as to the health of teachers, administrators, students, and other living things. It's also hazardous to fulfilling our purpose.

One heroic and insightful parent, mindful of the corrosive and demoralizing effect that relentless parent criticism was having on the school's culture, on the morale of teachers, and thereby on the learning experience of children, responded. She decided to write a little article each week in the school's take-home newsletter describing something especially noteworthy and praiseworthy she had experienced in the performance of a teacher that week.

At first this addition to the bake sales and athletic contests reported in the paper was little noticed. But not for long. Soon, other parents began to contribute to this column, and many more were reading it. Within a short time, these words of commendation had drawn attention to how much of worth was going on in the school. Teachers began to feel known, appreciated, and valued. And I am certain that, as a consequence, they began to approach their little rooms full of twenty-six lively bodies with new energy, heart, and determination.

These periodic, public words supporting the efforts of teachers were healing at first. Soon they became community building. After all, what is a community but a place full of people who care about, look after, and root for one another, who work together for the good of the whole, in times of need as well as times of celebration? In particular these written plaudits helped our school move closer to being the community of learners we all sought.

The story gives rise to **Working Rule 9:**

Acknowledge and applaud not only accomplishment but also effort.

These accolades, offered by parents to teachers, acknowledged usually small yet influential actions of teachers—an effort to give special help to a troubled student; creating a new, experiential curriculum for a group of students having difficulty with long division; setting up a volunteer service for parents to assist in classrooms. These were only efforts, not "results." They were not assurance of "profound learning" or instruments of admission to Harvard. But they mattered. A lot.

How much better to reflect than to attack. Encourage rather than demean. How much better to slowly fill the glass than to shatter it.

CHAPTER 10

Right or Wrong?

Soon after departing York Harbor, Donald went ashore and Snyder came aboard. With the aid of an excellent if venerable Esso gas station map (retrieved from the glove compartment of my 1931 Model A Ford), Snyder and I successfully navigated our way somewhere near Cape Elizabeth and put in for the night. I usually prefer a mooring, but after the night in York Harbor, an anchor offered greater peace of mind. I paddled ashore to inquire of our location and to search for some charts of the Maine coast. This journey was effected on my inflated air mattress, because we had lost the dinghy at sea. The mattress had also performed well the night before on top of my sleeping bag, keeping out the rain that paused only briefly on the leaky deck.

Now certain of our location and provisioned with proper charts, we set sail across Casco Bay. Our intended landfall was Potts Harbor on Harpswell Neck. Diligently following our compass, prudently installed directly over the decidedly ferrous gasoline engine, we attempted to relate its numbers to those of the compass rose on the chart. But why was one compass rose superimposed on another? The Esso map didn't have any! As we approached the east side of Casco Bay, the sun began to set. But we could see well enough to carefully match each of the many landmasses before us with each of the many symbols for land masses on the chart. Perfect! We knew where we were. As we closed in on the shore, the clues on the chart remained congruent with the reality before us—all but two. One navigation aid, N-4, appeared off our bow yet showed nowhere on the chart. Conversely, one navigation aid on the chart, R-2, was nowhere to be found with the binoculars.

Undeterred, and convinced we were where we thought we were—and, more important, where we *wanted* to be—we contemplated an explanation. After due deliberation we decided that the resourceful Town Fathers, in their inexplicable and ornery wisdom, had defied the Coast Guard and hauled R-2, probably to sell to a tourist, and had replaced it with N-4, probably surplus World War II stock they had kicking around. In the absence of any dissenting voices, our theory offered persuasive credibility.

Having dispatched these minor discrepancies to our satisfaction, we entered the harbor, neatly missing all of the ominous underwater rocks marked on the chart (the Esso map was both easier to use and created less anxiety). We tied up smartly at the dock beside a lobster boat and congratulated ourselves on successfully completing another leg of our voyage Down East.

It was only then that the huge sign over the fisherman's co-op came to our attention. It announced that we had arrived safely not at Potts Harbor but at Mackerel Cove, some two miles and two peninsulas to the south. That moment I was reminded of the words of Albert Einstein: "Only two things are infinite: the universe and human stupidity. And I'm not sure about the former."

In subsequent years, we have had occasion to question the presence, the absence, and the numbering system of navigation aids along the Maine coast that were not where or what they were supposed to be. And always we find comfort in attributing the discrepancies between what we see and what we should be seeing to the work of the Town Fathers, who, like gremlins, never rest.

The good news is that as the years pass, we are no longer quite so certain the Town Fathers Theory holds (deep) water; the bad news is that what the chart says *should* be there and what we observe *is* there continues to differ at alarming times and in alarming ways. Fortunately, always offering comfort has been **Cruising Rule 10:**

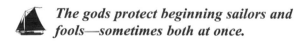

The gods protect beginning sailors and fools—sometimes both at once.

Recently, I asked a distinguished, well-attired yachtsman aboard a distinguished, well-traveled 40-foot sloop his "local knowledge" on passing safely through Bracketts Channel between Job Island and Islesboro. A solitary unmarked rock, two feet below mean low tide appears on the chart—and probably in the passage.

"You simply line up that dock with Tumbledown Dick Point, hoist all sails, crank up your engine to full throttle, shut off your depth finder, and proceed at hull speed. *I've* never had any trouble," he advised soberly.

Clearly, the gods protect others as well.

~~~~~~~~~

"**D**ad thought you'd like these."

Johnny, a fifth-grader, handed me an envelope. I opened it to discover, with delight, two tickets to the upcoming Boston Bruins game. Center ice!

As a beginning public school principal, I was vaguely aware of a regulation that forbade accepting gifts from parents. But this detail was easy to dismiss because I'd never been to a Bruins game, had always wanted to go, and tickets were unobtainable. Oh, why get wrapped up in bureaucratic details!

I accepted the tickets and that weekend enjoyed watching Bobby Orr score the winning goal, with seconds remaining, to defeat the Detroit Red Wings. My first NHL hockey game was a winner. I drove home so delighted that I had made the decision to keep the gift from Johnny's dad that I wrote him a thank you note.

"Dad wanted me to give you this."

It was Johnny again, a month later . . . with another envelope. This time I found inside, not a brace of Bruins tickets, but a brief sentence:

"My wife and I have decided that we would like Johnny to be in Mrs. Samson's class next year."

It was a simple enough request. Or was it a demand? Either way it's an easy matter for a principal to ensure that a Johnny have a Mrs. Samson for a teacher the upcoming year.

But there was a problem. A big problem. Placing each of seventy-five fifth-graders into each of three sixth-grade classes was hardly a simple matter. Before my arrival the process had been compromised and had become reduced to "The parent who screams the loudest and manipulates the most gets to pick." And favorites were played.

I had been working hard to bring some rationality—and integrity—to the process. Parents were now invited to write me a letter describing the conditions under which they felt their youngster best learned. I asked sending teachers to spend a day each winter visiting the classes of potential receiving teachers to become familiar with how they handled different kinds of youngsters. Then together, the teachers, school psychologist, and I made decisions that predicted the most promising match.

Only then did we read letters from parents to see if new information from them might suggest a different placement. But parents did *not* select their child's teacher. Nor did the principal.

But what if the naïve principal had previously accepted two Bruins tickets, acknowledged with a thank you note? Was he now beholden to the parents, and perhaps vulnerable, lest the parents disclose the principal had accepted—dare I say—a bribe?

To my consternation I realized that I had allowed myself to be placed in a most compromising dilemma. I could violate Johnny's parents' request and risk both exposing my violation of district policy and alienating the parents. I could wait for the teachers' recommended placement, which had a chance of complying with Johnny's parents' wishes. If this didn't work I could overrule the teachers and honor the request, which would only deepen my complicity and confirm to the parents that the tickets had indeed bought the preferred teacher. A message I hardly wanted to send.

None of these possible courses of action made me feel good about myself. I took a deep breath and wrote a note to Johnny's parents, reminding them (again) of our placement policy and process. I told them that this was a collaborative decision the faculty would make and I would approve, taking their letter into account.

Came the placement meeting, the teachers expressed strong feelings that Johnny would do best with Mr. Brown next year. We so notified Johnny's parents.

I was relieved—nay, overjoyed—that nothing further came of this matter. But I learned a lasting lesson, which is now **Working Rule 10:**

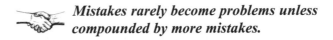 *Mistakes rarely become problems unless compounded by more mistakes.*

When you want something desperately enough, it's easy to ignore signals telling you that you shouldn't have it. Going on, in the face of evidence that suggests you not go on, leads down a perilous path. Not learning from our first mistake can make the next one fatal.

So now I tell myself, unless there's a darn good reason not to, "attend to policies"—and landmarks and navigation aids—even when they are contrary to what you wish they were—and where you wish you were. Put differently, I told myself "never do anything I don't want to read about on the front page of the *Boston Globe*!"

We cannot assume the gods will forever protect beginning principals—and fools.

Chapter 11

Held Harmless

Sailing involves an unending array of unexpected events, circumstances, and maneuvers that challenge the ability, resourcefulness, and judgment of the best. It is not uncommon, when the skill of the sailor comes up against the demands of the situation, for something aboard the vessel to break. Nothing is so destructive to the spirit of the mariner and to his relationship with his sailing companion as being held responsible, even blamed, for the damage. At the very least, conversation should always delicately consider whether the fault lies with human error or with a structural weakness.

Late one October, Snyder, his Coast Guardsman friend, and I were sailing *Moses Swann* around Pemaquid Point and up the Damariscotta River to be hauled for the winter. It was our last available weekend: Gotta do it! Unfortunately, the appointed weekend brought with it gale-force winds and treacherous seas.

Well offshore, *Moses* opened up some seams and began to take on water, a lot of green water. At first, the electric bilge pump maintained the balance of inflow with outflow. When the water in the bilge reached the battery, the Coast Guardsman was assigned to the manual guinea pump in the cockpit. When the water began gaining on us again, I went below with a bucket while Snyder, at the helm, tried to hold course.

Despite our heroic efforts, water continued to come in faster than we could bail it out. "That's the definition of sinking!" observed our guest from the United States Coast Guard, dryly.

Well off of Outer Heron Island and headed for Ireland, with engine swamped, battery under, and unable to come about in the

37

gale, I decided to gybe the huge mainsail of *Moses Swann*. The resulting cataclysm fractured the gaff jaws, parted the main throat halyard, and snapped the gaff in two. Ah yes, as the saying goes, "That which does not destroy us makes us stronger."

How heartening, therefore, to hear from my sailing partner that windy day on Muscongus Bay, "You know, Roland, these old wooden gaff rigs just don't hold up in a gybe. I guess that's why the world switched over to the Marconi rig." Now *that* is the stuff of a lasting relationship, and an excellent predictor that (once the damage is repaired) another "boys' night on the town" will take place. And therein lies **Cruising Rule 11:**

> *Any damage incurred by a vessel is due to a deficiency in the equipment and not to the judgment or competence of the individual involved.*

Moses limped back into New Harbor, whereupon a freshly installed battery powered the pump once again, emitting a comforting hum all night long. Nevertheless, we slept with arms draped into the bilge as water detectors—just in case.

Have you ever ruined a white shirt by washing it with colored clothes in hot water? How about that colleague who spilled coffee on your computer keyboard? And what about that dent sustained in my car door when I backed into a telephone pole as I emerged from a distressing visit to my tax accountant? Damn!

Damage, while usually far less devastating than broken rigging in a gale, seems to occur at every turn of our lives. And repairing damage seems to be a full-time job. I have come to believe wholeheartedly the adage, "to err is human."

Yet it isn't the physical damage that takes the major toll on our lives. Most damage of that sort can be fixed, mended, or replaced. It is our *reaction* to ourselves, to others, and to these infuriating incidents that takes the larger toll. Our often impulsive reactions can quickly lead to personal and interpersonal damage. And, as we know, personal and interpersonal carnage is far more difficult to fix, mend, or heal.

Snyder could have easily snapped at my mistake and assigned warranted blame. And such a response would have placed our relationship at risk—in addition to the already-plentiful risk we faced at sea. But he didn't. Instead, the day ended—mercifully—with my appreciation for his support and a deepened friendship. And, to the astonishment of the Coast Guardsman, there was no admiralty inquiry!

This heavy weather experience taps into a rule that transcends the confines of a ship's cabin. Indeed, **Working Rule 11** serves us all well in our work together:

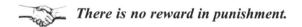 *There is no reward in punishment.*

How we respond to trying, extreme, or unexpected circumstances calls upon us to accept in others what we often have difficulty accepting in ourselves. Mistakes. I can accidentally dent the car door and drive home awash in a stream of self-inflicted invectives (in fact, I am still punishing myself for that dent, now long-since repaired). But if my daughter creases a fender backing out of the garage, how much better to reassure her that the car is getting old, now no one will want to steal it, and I wanted to replace it anyway.

We need to bring more generosity of spirit and a sense of proportion to our own mistakes, and especially to the modest transgressions of others. It is as difficult as it is important to comfort others and to reassure them when they damage something of value to us. "Human feelings are frail, the ways of the world are rugged," Zen tells us.

In the end, relationships are more important than making sure blame and guilt are thoroughly assigned. A stained shirt, a computer keyboard, and a car door—even a splintered gaff—are reparable. To err is human, but it is to *forgive* that is divine. Or, as my wife Barbara once told me, "Hey, cut me a little slack here!"

Chastising and judging are usually a reaction, offered up in anger, frustration, and exasperation. The person doing the scolding will inevitably feel remorse; the person on the receiving end will smart from the incident for a long, long while. And their relationship will become guarded, strained, and emotionally remote.

Not that we should hold ourselves—or others—"harmless" from *every* mistake. There are misdeeds we commit (such as those Boston Bruins tickets!) that should cause us to take a hard and critical look at errant behavior and *not* accept, dismiss, or deflect it. But the bulk of transgressions made by us and by others does not warrant such severe treatment.

When we come to recognize ourselves in the mistakes of others and respond with understanding and compassion, our relationships will continue not only to stay afloat, but to sail!

CHAPTER 12

On Balance

For too many years, sailing meant not only doing it, doing all of it, but overdoing all of it. We virile males pushed and horsed vessel, crew, guests, and ourselves not only to full capabilities, but also well beyond until something physical or interpersonal broke. "Testing limits," I believe counselors of adolescents call it.

When we got our first sloop, we noticed that the mainsail was adorned with three rows of rather quaint pieces of rope. It took us several seasons to learn what they did . . . and it took another season to learn how to do it. It took even more to actually do it.

We learned that these pieces of rope are called reef points. On a sailboat, as in a car, it is possible to adjust the power according to conditions. The prudent sailor would no more try to sail through heavy winds with full sail up than a sensible driver would move through heavy traffic with full throttle down.

The three sets of reef points enable a vessel to shorten sail and be appropriately suited to roughly 20, 30, or 40 knots of wind. Otherwise, you ship lots of water over the side or break something. If that happens, both vessel and relationships may be severely damaged.

Only once have I ever set out with a triple reef. That was when David came from Alaska for his first (and thus far, only) sail on the Maine coast. Unfortunately, his one available October day found it blowing a gale. Therefore, we set out.

Suddenly, we found ourselves in the midst of a snow squall. We struggled to find Round Pond in the approaching darkness—a simultaneous whiteout and blackout. Once we located the harbor, we had to locate the considerably smaller mooring. Just as David found the mooring, the prop found the pennant. "Oh dear," I said politely. To unwind the mess, I dove, naked as a jaybird, from the white deck into the whitecaps. I have not employed three reefs since.

It was only after two decades of living in this state of arrested development—cruising with too much sail up, too little ballast down, too much seawater over the gunwales and into the cockpit, too many numbing rainy days, too much terrifying fog, too many broken gaff jaws, and too many rough passages accompanied by too much lunch lost overboard—that we made an important discovery: One can deliberately choose to avoid excess. It is possible not to subject self, others, and vessel to the punishing, brutal, uncomfortable, and unsafe experiences that lie in endless supply offshore.

It was then that we discovered a New World that forever transformed our lives at sea. We had landed upon what is now known as the "Comfort Factor."

At first, of course, this was a discovery made in the names of women and children. While others reveled in the new order, we men merely tolerated sanity at sea. But now, when faced with a decision about whether to set out, to motor rather than sail, to reef, to hang it up for the day at cocktail hour rather than groping in the dark, we have begun to hear ourselves say, "Let's consider the Comfort Factor." By doing so we have enshrined **Cruising Rule 12:**

 *Reef early and often.*

It has dawned on us that a version of the Boston ward heeler's political advice, "Vote early and often," may also be good nautical advice. At sea, you can't control the winds, but you can control the sails.

In the workplace everyone is capable of his or her best—and worst. I used to think of my responsibility as leader of the school as engaging in the intriguing exercise of discovering—and then providing—conditions under which every member of the school community—teachers, students, parents, and myself—would give their best most of the time. A novel and worthwhile activity to be sure.

What are the conditions that elicit the best in us most of the time? For some it is a kick in the pants; for others a pat on the back. For some exacting, detailed expectations, deadlines, and accountability; for yet others, "academic freedom." For some, working alone; for others, functioning as team members.

One football coach will have jaw-smashing scrimmages for eight hours for the six days before the big game. His assumption is that the team will be tough, ready, prepared and relieved when the forced march is over and the relatively manageable game conditions actually arrive.

Another coach orders up a day of films and strategies on Monday; a full scrimmage on Tuesday and Wednesday; light workouts without pads on Thursday and Friday; and a day off on Saturday for players to spend with families and friends. His assumption: They will be rested, ready, and happy.

These two teams and coaches raise questions about what is optimal. How hard to push? Do you proceed with full sail up or with a reef or two? Which team would you rather play on? For which coach would you give your best efforts? Which team is better prepared to win?

These examples suggest that in the workplace, although we can seldom control our purpose, we can always influence how we go about fulfilling it.

The common work culture is characterized by the following credos:

The more the better.

The faster the better.

The sooner the better.

The better the better.

It's all too easy to push a business, a team, a colleague, ourselves, to full capacity and well beyond full capacity—until something physical or interpersonal breaks. When an important project must be out the door by Friday we go 24/7. We "horse" it and we horse those around us. We're busy, we're exhausted, and we're pulled in too many directions at once. Everything in excess: coffee, sleepless all-nighters, all the while oblivious to family, health, and working relationships.

Everything in excess—except balance.

Many organizations and individuals have yet to discover *their* reefing points, which would enable them to match their capacity to the conditions around them. To be sure, sometimes our work gives us no choice.

We could all use **Working Rule 12:**

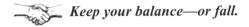 *Keep your balance—or fall.*

We pride ourselves on our productivity. But just as there are costs of low productivity, there are costs of high productivity. In the workplace, as on a sailing vessel, it is possible to deliberately choose to avoid excess. By this I don't mean substituting for a culture of the forced march a culture of undisciplined frivolity, fun, and games. The workplace *is,* after all, about productivity; it is not about comfort.

I find a definition of leadership shared with me by Dennis Perkins both helpful and compelling: "a leader is one who accomplishes the goals of the organization without sacrificing core values."

This conception contrasts with the working definition I observe in most organizations, which is "Accomplish the goals of the organization . . . at all costs." They've got the first part right. But the second part wrong.

In schools, for instance, commonly espoused core values often include honesty, teamwork, cooperation, shared leadership, and integrity. Yet the press these days is all too replete with stories of schools accomplishing their goals (e.g., bringing scores on standardized tests up to snuff) but doing so by nefarious means. A principal excludes the scores of the special education students. One teacher prepares students for tests using purloined test items. Another erases incorrect student marks and inflates test scores.

Other organizations have their distinctive core values—and regularly violate them in the name of accomplishing their goals. Recent scandals in the corporate business world, for instance, have caused us to lose confidence and respect in the way they "do business."

Profits appear to be up but so is deceit. The Catholic Church offers another painful example.

So what happened to honesty, teamwork, and integrity?

We must become clear about just what goals we wish to accomplish. We must become clear about what core values we wish to instill in our workplaces and in ourselves. We must take these goals and values seriously. And, above all, we must take the values as seriously as the goals. When we do, I believe we will be on our way to bringing out the best in others, in ourselves, and in our organizations . . . most of the time.

CHAPTER 13

Loose Lips

S hortly after the near sinking of the *Moses Swann* and in defer-
ence to the Comfort Factor, we formed yet a third syndicate and
purchased a rebuilt, 1911, 35-foot original Friendship sloop. She had
the graceful lines of a swan, but not the name. Neither deck nor hull
leaked; her diesel engine worked; and she was already handsomely
attired in cat's-ass brindle. A twenty-year love affair had begun.

The story went that her name derived from the alcoholic habits
of an owner in the '30s who was partial to a high-octane, New
Orleans–blended whisky. Each summer, he imported a case to Maine
to accompany him on his foggy cruises. One day a friend nailed to
the transom a slat from that case with the word "Sazerac" branded
on it. *Sazerac* she has been ever since.

On a bright, spring day *Sazerac* was launched, freshly painted,
oiled, and varnished by Paul Bryant's capable hands. She looked
like a million dollars. Three of us—Snyder, me, and another owner,
who shall remain nameless—sailed her up Muscongus Sound to
Round Pond. Now, there are only two submerged impediments
between Pemaquid Point and Round Pond. Poland North Ledge,
waiting patiently just below water level and prominently marked by
a large can buoy, is one of them.

On that fateful day, when the wind died, the third owner started
the engine, took the helm, and powered us along at six knots—all the
while engrossed in his own erudite lecture on the sinking of the
Lusitania. Snyder and I went forward to furl the generous mainsail.
Suddenly, the Comfort Factor and our cushioned world of the sea
were rudely replaced by an 8.2 Richter-scale jolt. As upper fillings

fell to the deck, *Sazerac* lurched over on her beam and ground to an indelicate halt—square atop Poland North Ledge. Neither proper chart nor Esso map were anywhere to be found. Bright green C-3 glistened not ten yards away. "Right, red, return," indeed! Necessity called upon us to immediately craft **Cruising Rule 13:**

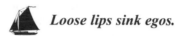 ***Loose lips sink egos.***

We agreed that in the rare event that damage to the craft is sustained due to undeniably and inescapably human error, lack of judgment, or just plain stupidity, no discussion of the incident by those who witnessed it shall occur at the time or thereafter. Most especially, nothing will ever be disclosed to those ashore.

The rock has since been locally renamed "_____ Mistake" in honor of that hapless helmsperson.

~~~~~~~~

My neighbor Nigel is an unusually accomplished sailor and author. He has sailed more seas and written more cruising guides and books about various aspects of boating than anyone I know of.

On the very day he submitted the manuscript for his new book, *How to Read a Nautical Chart,* he was at the helm of a friend's brand-new catamaran, breezing along at seven knots, with chart in hand. His reverie was suddenly interrupted by a tremendous jolt and the gnashing of fiberglass. They had fetched up on East Haddock Ledge; another of Muscongus Bay's many hidden wonders. The damage to vessel—and ego—was severe. The potential damage to his friendship with the vessel's owner, who was also aboard, was even greater.

What Nigel chose to do was instructive. To everyone's astonishment, rather than deep-sixing this unfathomable event, which reflected poorly on him as a seafaring man (as I confess I might have been tempted to do), he chose to write an article about it for publication in a leading sailing magazine!

By coming clean he accomplished many things:

He forced himself to analyze the unpleasant event in detail and figure out how this could have happened—to *him*. What he would rather render forgettable became unforgettable.

And in the process he learned some things about chart reading and navigating the coast of Maine, which he had not known (I suspect these revelations will appear in the second edition).

Next he disclosed to others what he had learned, thus alerting and warning them, and making it less likely that *they* would follow in his wake and repeat his mistakes.

Furthermore, he decided that compensation for this article would pay for restoring the hull—and friendship.

And finally, and perhaps most important, he telegraphed the message to all of us sailors, that while "gods may protect beginning sailors and fools," they do not protect experts. Rather, it is precisely when you—or others—believe that you are an expert that you may be most at risk. As Winston Churchill once said, "We will not make the mistakes of the past; our mistakes will be bigger and better."

In short, rather than become preoccupied with maintaining his image and ego, Nigel chose to learn from his mistake and convey this learning to fellow sailors.

So Cruising Rule 13 should probably be changed to **Working Rule 13:**

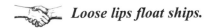 *Loose lips float ships.*

Although it may be humiliating to make public one's screwups, it is irresponsible to withhold them from one's colleagues, destined to make the same mistake.

The medical profession is well known for its "M and M rounds." Mortality and morbidity. This time-honored practice requires that physicians and physicians-in-training meet regularly, reveal and examine in detail all cases that result in a patient's death or medical complication. Rather than "bury their mistakes," doctors find it their moral obligation to their profession, to their patients, and to their colleagues to disclose and learn from mistakes and unfavorable outcomes. It is a low road, indeed, to preserve one's ego at the expense of colleagues' learning and patients' lives.

Good performance is important; learning publicly from poor performance is even more important.

CHAPTER 14

Fatal Attraction

Boats accumulate stuff. Lots of it. Understandably. For, when you are in the middle of the ocean, desperately in need of a piece of equipment—a rigging knife, a socket wrench, an alternator belt, toilet paper—it had better be on board. Yet somehow, something is always missing. Therefore, skippers maintain lists of those items so they may be added to the ship's provisions when next ashore. In this way, the amount of stuff soon expands to fill—and exceed—the amount of space allotted for its storage.

Aboard ship, an infinite number of pieces of equipment constantly challenge the finite number of spaces. Thus, a sailing vessel becomes a floating closet that carefully holds a variety of equipment used only occasionally, if at all. It's no wonder the area below is referred to as "the hold." Lockers, shelves, cupboards, lazarettes, cabinets, and compartments are built to conform to peculiar hull shapes and sizes. Into these are stored objects of congruent, peculiar shapes and sizes. Every skipper, therefore, must be severe, selective, and yet prescient about what comes aboard. Anything allowed to make the trip from dock to deck must have a clear purpose.

On a sailing vessel, for some curious reason, the vast majority of equipment stowed above and below deck is heavier than water. Put differently, it sinks. On my boat only two pieces of equipment are deliberately designed for this—the lead line and the anchor. And both are best, but not always, deployed when attached to a cleat. Only one piece of equipment —the life preserver—seems to have been deliberately designed to float, although we used to carry some old ones used as fenders that did sink. To be completely honest, a

49

zucchini also does float—barely. But I'm not sure it was deliberately designed to. However, by some perverted law of nature and Neptune, the rest seems inexplicably drawn to the sea bottom.

Day or night, under sail or power, at anchor or moored, a magically magnetic force seems constantly to beckon the contents of my floating closet, inviting them to leave their safe, dry, warm resting grounds and to enter the wet, cold, and unknown ocean. I call it the "Fatal Attraction."

Unfortunately, as all sailors know, quite frequently these non-buoyant pieces of gear don't just abandon ship, they eagerly succumb to what my gastrointestinal physician calls a "sense of urgency." They leap joyfully over the side.

Take prescription sunglasses. The mooring stone in Round Pond is sprinkled liberally with expensive, carefully ground optical wear, which sprung from my nose into the waters below as I lunged for the buoy, amidst flogging jib and lurching sea. Then, of course, there are the tools—socket wrenches, sockets, pliers, crescent wrenches—used to service the outboard, remove a cotter pin, repair an oarlock. Usually midway through any project (never upon its completion) the tool, with a mind of its own, decides that it would prefer life at the bottom, rather than the top, of the sea. I remember one night the veritable joy with which my new waterproof flashlight jumped from my grasp as it beautifully illuminated the anchor rope. It then slowly and gracefully twirled through the water, offering an eerie light and watery pirouette all the way down. Its lifetime Eveready batteries no doubt continue to brighten some lobster's lair.

And clothing. How many hats, gloves, shirts, and towels have caught a good puff and leapt overboard? I remember my daughter Carolyn's new red shorts that went directly from ship's locker to Davy Jones's locker, without even pausing on my daughter.

And, of course, there is the silverware. When one is washing dishes in the cockpit, usually after supper in the dark, the last remnants of the dirty, soapy water are happily dispatched over the side. No matter how carefully the bucket of dishwater is inspected, it always seems to contain eating implements. We have now learned to be content with forgettable American Airlines forks and spoons that my resourceful mother liberated from a 727 years ago.

And there is that piece of nautical gear, never found on a proper Friendship sloop, but with which I have recently become acquainted—the winch handle. I've seen "floating winch handles" advertised, but I've never seen one of my winch handles float. When urgently shifted from port to starboard to crank the unruly jibsheet, they literally spring from the hand's tightened grip and execute perfect one and one-half gainers into the briny pool.

Snyder and I speculate that if the plug on Muscongus Bay were pulled and the water drained, an extraordinary sedimentary deposit would be revealed: wrenches, winch handles, spoons, forks, eyeglasses, caps, gloves, shoes, towels, nuts, bolts, iron, copper, brass, and stainless from every seagoing vessel since Captain John Smith's best astrolabe abandoned ship in 1605. Enough stuff to equip handsomely every boat on the coast of Maine, we figure.

For years we fought a losing battle. We tried to restrain these magnetic urges. Straps on glasses, binoculars, hand-bearing compass; lines, lanyards, and pennants (even buoyed pennants on endangered crescent wrenches) were to no avail. The more we worried about dropping a screwdriver overboard while at work on the transom rubrail, the more precautions taken not to lose the only brass pin while out on the bowsprit hooking up the forestay, the more tightly our teeth grasped cotter pins, the more certain became their inevitable, irreversible seaward trajectory.

These many losses overboard have also caused unbelievable stress to onboard relationships. I remember once under sail when my daughter's boyfriend dropped a piece of the ship's "finest" dinnerware overboard. This caused some palpable, if unstated, stress aboard. Miraculously, the bowl floated. As we made a pass to retrieve the precious object, the young man grabbed for it, touched it, and sank it. This unfortunate casualty caused some now-stated stress among all permutations of father, boyfriend, and daughter. It is at such times that human bodies have come close to following equipment overboard. That is, until the gods revealed **Cruising Rule 14:**

 The rightful resting place for every piece of equipment on board is at the bottom of the sea.

It has now dawned on us that the reason most of the ship's stuff sinks is that it *belongs* down there, every bit as much as the cod and haddock, just as birds fly because they belong *up* there. It is their natural habitat. Life of the ship's gear aboard is aberrant and ephemeral, each item awaiting its earliest opportunity to go home.

We no longer begrudge the winch handle its rightful home. Its true purpose in life is to lounge in the dark mud, beneath eight fathoms of seawater, not work in the glare atop a chrome winch head. We have no business, no right, preventing it from going home. It *will* go home anyway.

Since we ceased cleverly clasping the crescent wrench, since I stopped worrying about depositing yet another $100 pair of glasses atop the mooring, since we stopped anxiously masticating cotter pins, less seems to have fallen or jumped overboard. Not even the rusting American Airlines spoons. I wish they would.

~~~~~~~~~

Work is an essential part of our being. We want and need to work—to feed, clothe and shelter ourselves and our families, to give purpose to our lives, to contribute to the world in which we live, and, not least, to acquire possessions that provide us pleasure, distraction, status, and comfort.

Things. Material items serve many purposes in our lives, even if the purpose is only to whet our appetite for more. A friend of mine, who owns more boats than I, once offered, "The one who dies with the most toys wins!"

We in this wealthy nation work desperately to earn income so that we can buy, buy, and buy some more. A walk through the mall reveals around us an almost rapacious and insatiable appetite to accumulate more. And we do. We are faced with an overwhelming array of choices. The corresponding inventory of electronic goods, items in the wardrobe, and adult toys in our households is staggering.

And because we have been so successful in accumulating more and more things, we create for ourselves another problem: Where do we put it all? On a boat, when something is lost at sea we must relinquish, let go. There is a certain finality about no longer having that crescent wrench.

On land, however, when gravity exerts its pull, when we "lose" something, it is still there ... only we don't know where. So we have to keep looking for it and become frustrated when we can't find it. There is no relief from our surfeit of stuff.

We may not live on a boat, but the space allotted for storage is nonetheless finite. There isn't room for another suit on the rack or car in the garage or appliance on the counter. We drown in our own excess and clutter. So we build additions or buy larger homes. Or store stuff in rented self-storage bays. The problem of "how can I earn enough to purchase more," once transcended, begets other more complex problems. How can I store it, keep track of it, protect it, maintain it, and develop a retrieval system so I can find it when I want it.

So we must invent elaborate categories in our lives that enable us to live, while swamped with stuff: "keep out and ready to use often," like the microwave. "Keep on an accessible shelf where it can be used occasionally," like the blender. "Store in the basement or attic where it may be used, occasionally, when we want it" like the Christmas tree stand. "Take up to the summer place and store in the barn for the grandchildren," like the old high chair.

Computers allow us to "save" and hoard even more effectively. And they demand that we discard less. Yet their very capacity only adds to the net growth of files and folders of which we must now somehow keep track.

Because we must reconcile our relentless acquisitiveness with a finite amount of space, we must divest. Because we cannot depend upon Davy Jones for help in relieving us of our excess of possessions, we develop a complex calculus, which goes like this: "Give away to a friend who is looking for one," like the bread maker we no longer use. "Give away to Good Will" like the unwanted three-speed bike. "Throw into the garbage," like the chipped salad bowl. And so it goes.

At home or in the workplace we might better address problems of storing, maintaining, losing, or divesting things on the front end— by not accumulating them in the first place. Because, no matter how we categorize and divest ourselves of stuff, it creeps back in and threatens to choke our lives like the insatiable kudzu vine. The line between need and want becomes increasingly blurred.

It isn't wrong to want and to value things. Things can make our lives easier, more comfortable, and more satisfying. What can be wrong is placing a high value on material possessions at the expense of other, more important "things"—spending time with family and friends, contributing to the community, developing our own learning. One wise grandmother advised her grandchild to spend one third of her life earning, one third serving, and one third learning. Makes sense to me!

In our efforts to safeguard our stuff, we must be careful that we not lose or have taken from us something of greater value: our connections with those we cherish.

Why did I fear losing that plastic plate at sea more than I feared losing my daughter's affection and her friend's respect?

Why do we want to have a fancier car than the "Joneses" when by winning this competition we diminish our friendship with them?

Why is acquiring a new wardrobe more important than deepening friendship with those who may admire us wearing it?

Regularly losing numerous objects overboard has forced me to confront the concept of "letting go." Relinquishing material possessions can be strangely liberating, even cleansing. It causes me to reflect on other things in my life that I might want to let go: coveting my friend's forty-two-foot sloop; the feeling of irritation at my daughter's boyfriend; and my impatience with myself in attempting to master the computer.

The best we bring to our friends, family, colleagues, and ourselves is often jeopardized by the predominant place we accord our things and possessions. Our attractions to material objects can easily become fatal attractions.

Which leads us to **Working Rule 14:**

 Be careful what you work for.

I find myself asking with greater and greater frequency these days, "How much is enough?"

How many pairs of sneakers? How many boats? How many radios and clocks and cameras and binoculars and computers and lamps and pillows and tractors and mowers and saws and hammers? How much is enough?

Our predicament is not, of course, new. As the industrial revolution was just beginning to churn out consumer goods, that wonderful sage of Concord, Henry David Thoreau, offered advice, as timely today as it was more than a century ago:

Simplify.

Simplify.

Simplify.

CHAPTER 15

Going It Together

I've never had much luck at fishing. However, this hasn't deterred my everlasting hopefulness and the fantasies that accompany putting on the fisherman's hat. Despite the perils inherent in mixing hooks, lines, and sinkers with mainsheets, jibsheets, and staysail sheets, I have mounted several memorable fishing expeditions under sail.

One drama searching for groundfish was cast off Pumpkin Ledge. Albert, the most passionate and accomplished fisherman known to me, and no doubt to fish, hooked onto a Big One and fought courageously for an hour, only to discover our huge cod was a modest lobster trap. Later that day, lowering our aspirations, we switched to mackerel. We chased a school into Browns Cove and soon loaded up a mackerel rig with five very live ones. Unfortunately, as they came over the gunwale, the line snapped and we parted company. Off they went, in perfect synchrony. "The Rockettes," Albert observed, ruefully.

Another occasion, however, stands out from the rest. Not one, but two Big Ones were boated. Sort of. Harold and I set out on a serious bluefish quest. We had heard they were feeding in Muscongus Bay and were determined to get our share. After a quiet night at anchor on Burnt Island, we arose with the morning light, an incoming tide, and a light breeze. Optimistically trolling two squidlike lures on fifty-pound tackle, we rounded Old Woman Ledge. Suddenly Harold yelled, "I've got one!" And he did. As his pole doubled over and he strained to hang on, I tried to luff up. At that instant, *I* got one! I immediately experienced a deficit of hands and feet, as I did my ineffectual best to attend to Harold, throw off the sheets, grab the helm, hang onto my fishing rod, reel in, and maintain contact with a now severely canted, pitching deck.

Our quarry crisscrossed in *Sazerac*'s wake and found and fouled one another several yards astern. The sloop, without helmsman or crew, came about, gybed, luffed, ran, and went through its entire repertoire of points of sail as it tried to shake off the two bluefish— and the two blue fishermen. Somehow, we held onto the rods, the rods held onto the fish, and *Sazerac* held onto us all. With yet another hand, we brought the dinghy, *Jedediah,* up hard against the transom and together reeled the tangled, turbulent rat's nest of lures, line, and fish alongside—and up into the dinghy. Squinting through tears of laughter and satisfaction, we observed two thrashingly hand-some twenty-plus-pound blues. We gasped for breath—all four of us. The excitement and the novelty of actually *landing* two real fish overcame the exhaustion, but not the absurdity of our predicament.

After congratulating ourselves on our distinguished skills as fishermen, we turned to the next task at hand: getting the hooks out of these toothy creatures and the lines untangled, so we could get back into that school.

Harold gave the command for me to go aboard *Jedediah* to tend the fish. I ordered him to do the same. After a few seconds of sustained paralysis, we flipped for it. Harold lost. As I tried to keep the now over-sailed vessel under control in an increasing wind and sea, he stepped from the afterdeck of *Sazerac* onto the dinghy below. A swell suddenly changed the relative positions of all three, and his foot came down on the rail of the dinghy. Over they went: dinghy, Harold, and two con-fused fish. The dinghy, port side under, swamped. Harold lurched amidships, somehow righting *Jedediah.* Both emerged from the capsize nearly full of water. Harold had joined the now-replenished bluefish in a very lively seawater bathtub.

The voracious fish now had Harold in their element, rather than he having them in his. The ridiculous spectacle of the situation was exceeded only by the look of alarm on Harold's face. Somehow the Comfort Factor had vanished as he tried to stand his ground, knee deep in brine, valiantly defending the bow of the dinghy—and his life—with an oar, in a pitching sea, against two slashing, ferocious, and unhappy creatures wielding sharp, triple-ganged hooks.

Suffice it to say, through several acts of heroism, and even more of luck, we won and the blues lost. They were consumed with relish for dinner that night (along with the "long version"). But they did not die in vain, for they bequeathed to us **Cruising Rule 15:**

 Be careful who you get into a boat with.

~~~~~~~~

T hat day at sea catching bluefish, while happily one of a kind, revealed with devastating clarity the perils and possibilities of teams and of teamwork. What we experienced plays out all too often in the workplace when colleagues attempt to work together toward a common end. The world of work is full of struggling teams trying ineptly to land their bluefish. Despite their best efforts, most of them come up against what Harold and I confronted:

1. Finding ourselves together in a confined space for an extended period of time.

2. Having a goal or an objective, which appears clear.

3. Making plans and preparations that we believe will be sufficient to handle whatever may come, as we move toward our objective.

4. Encountering the unexpected—suddenly.

5. Needing, in the moment, a clear set of new plans and clear resolution about who will do what and in what sequence.

6. Lacking clarity about who is in charge.

7. Struggling for leadership.

8. Realizing that risks must be taken . . . and that someone must take them.

9. Acting—and reacting—precipitously, under pressures of time and circumstance.

10. Experiencing unanticipated disasters as things continue to go awry.

11. Facing a sudden need for "damage control" with the event—and with one's colleagues.

12. All the while trying to keep in the forefront our primary objective.

Teamwork. So essential to any successful organization, school, or family. Yet assembling together around a table a school improvement team consisting of two teachers, two students, a principal, two parents, and two community members does not a team make. It makes two teachers, two students, a principal, two parents, and two community members! So how do you transform a bunch of bright, willful, pigheaded people into a highly performing team? This is a question subject to endless discussion in every human endeavor. Most teams are far better at generating conflict than at resolving it.

I think our day at sea, for all of its ridiculous and hilarious moments, may again be instructive. We can learn much from a "debrief" of the bluefish story, which can help develop more highly functioning teams. If Harold and I could do it over again, what would we do differently? Several things:

1. Become acquainted—first. Go through some simulated experiences *together* to become familiar with one another under battle conditions.

2. Before setting out, become clear, *together,* about just what the goal is.

3. Walk through, *together,* all of the known, potential scenarios that could be encountered and how to respond to them.

4. Take inventory, *together,* of one another's strengths and weaknesses that are relevant to the task at hand.

5. On the basis of these abilities—and disabilities—assign roles. *Together.* Who will do what?

6. Clarify, *together,* who is to be the leader of what activities. And what responsibilities will accompany the leader . . . and the followers?

7. Share leadership *together.*

8. Expect the unexpected; decide *together* how to respond to surprise.

9. Expect conflict; decide *together* what process will be employed to address and resolve conflict.

10. After the work has been completed, reflect on it *together.* How did it go? How well did each party address steps 1 through 9? What can we learn from this for use next time?

11. Celebrate successes, whatever they may have been, *together.*

And attend to **Working Rule 15:**

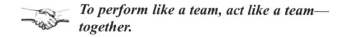 ***To perform like a team, act like a team— together.***

I have found the following probing debrief of attempts to work together as teammates particularly revelatory and helpful in building, by successive approximation, high performing teams. Periodically, members reflect in writing on the topics that follow. Then they consider *together* each response. Under this kind of honest examination most teams—even dysfunctional ones—learn and improve, *together.*

What I learned about my team from this experience is . . .

Some strengths that emerged from within the team are . . .

Did leadership emerge? From where?

What we need to work on to improve our team is . . .

What I need to work on to improve my contribution to our team is . . .

I would describe my part in this activity as:

Observer

Follower

Leader

Contributor

Obstructer

Other

Try it!

When clear goals have been established and members of the team are committed to them, when roles have been assigned on the basis of strengths and everyone is clear about their responsibilities and the job they are to do, when surprising events are expected and responded to, when conflict is addressed, and when members work *together,* team formation and improved performance is underway.

Then we won't have to be so careful who we get into a boat with!

CHAPTER 16

Captain's Orders

As the bluefish story attests, things happen suddenly at sea. Sometimes a man falls overboard, a keel bumps up on a ledge, a squall makes up. When a crisis erupts, the true sailor immediately and instinctively takes command, displays authority, and exerts leadership. The obvious indicator that this is occurring is the issuance of orders. Many of them. Rapidly. When, however, there are two or more sailors on board, particularly if co-owners, it is likely that each will immediately and instinctively take command, display authority, exert leadership, and give orders. Many of them. Rapidly. It is said that "We find comfort from those who agree with us, growth from those who do not." Perhaps this is why sailing produces so much growth.

Leadership is one of the most important and least understood of all phenomena. This much we know: For there to be a leader, there must be a follower. When there are two or more captains aboard, the leadership each inflicts upon the other places both at risk. If it cannot be democratically determined just which partner is the Captain, it could spoil a whole day. Even an entire relationship. Hence, the institution of **Cruising Rule 16:**

 Too many captains spoil the brine.

"Share leadership. Together." Easier said than done. Shared leadership is an elusive notion. It's difficult to describe, to define, to exhibit, and it's even more difficult to get team members to exhibit.

The world is still full of leaders like one old English headmaster who, when asked if he was democratic, replied, "Of course. I make no distinctions between the faculty and the boys—they are all my children."

Yet the day, if it ever existed, when a solitary, heroic figure can ride on a white horse into a business, a school, or other organization, and rescue it, has gone. Ample research suggests that a flourishing organization is one where "we" is used frequently and advisedly in spoken and written interactions.

Conversely, a heavy use of "I" is correlated with floundering organizations. Hierarchical, paternalistic work cultures beget workers who are heard to say, "I'd rather be a big part of the problem than a small part of the solution." Or, as Frank Lloyd Wright put it, "Beware of building from the top down."

We all have a need to be important, to be influential, to be recognized for our talents. When these needs are not met in positive ways, we are gifted at getting them met in negative ways.

Everyone wants to lead

One definition of leadership that I like very much is "making happen what you believe in." *Everyone* who works in an organization believes in something, and wants to make it happen. For instance in a school, teachers, students, principal, and parents all hold strong views about education and want to realize them.

A workplace can fulfill no higher purpose than to unlock those beliefs and desires and enable everyone to become the leader who lies within. And to help everyone to learn how to be a follower as well. All will benefit: leaders, colleagues, and the organization.

Everyone can lead

Organizations are overfull of underutilized talent. I have never met a person who was not capable of leadership. Perhaps not leadership of the whole group. Perhaps not leadership of an entire division or office. But leadership of some important portion of the organization. Everyone has the capacity to share his or her talent and contribute to the work of the whole. Some may be uncertain, lacking in confidence or leadership skills, but all have the stuff within them. Work cultures can be more or less friendly to widespread leadership. Some cultures expect it, encourage it, value it, and promote it in all employees. They get it. Others don't.

Leaders of organizations who succeed in promoting leadership in others become not "heroes" but "hero makers." As Ralph Nader once said, "The true measure of a leader is not how many followers you beget but how many leaders you beget."

Everyone should lead—and follow

Many organizations are beset with problems of "too many chiefs and not enough Indians." This is usually not a problem of excessive leadership, but rather of how to *manage* an organization with so many leaders. We're not very good at that.

And there is another problem. We are not very good at being followers of other people's lead. I remember working late in my principal's office one afternoon. Three third-grade youngsters came up on their bikes, outside my window. After a brief conversation, two of them suddenly pedaled off. Whereupon the third, about two feet high in stature, called after them, forlornly, "Hey, wait for me. I'm your leader!"

The difficulties of working through the knotty issues of managing multiple leaders and becoming skillful at following the lead of others, formidable as they are, pale beside the difficulties of trying to build and sustain a healthy, productive work culture with two classes of citizens: few leaders and many followers.

I am committed to the concept of a school as a "Community of Leaders," a place whose very mission is to unlock the leadership that lies latent within members of the community for the good of the whole. "A community is like a ship," Henrik Ibsen once suggested, "everyone ought to be prepared to take the helm."

Which gives rise to **Working Rule 16:**

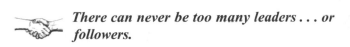 ***There can never be too many leaders . . . or followers.***

The power and necessity of shared leadership has never been clearer to me than when I met with a couple of dozen New Jersey school principals, shortly after September 11, 2001. Most of them presided over schools in the vicinity of the Twin Towers, some in view of them. The lives of many in these school communities were intricately linked with the lives—and deaths—across the Hudson River.

As these school leaders reflected on what happened that morning in their schools, what they faced, what they did, and how it went, one pervasive theme stood out: shared leadership. Not one acted or led alone. Most schools had "crisis management teams" that empowered and institutionalized leadership in members of the school community. To be sure, these administrators exercised strong leadership. But in addition, parents stepped up to the plate making sure each child returned to a home where an adult was present; teachers stepped up to the plate and covered for their colleagues who went in search of their loved ones; students stepped up to the plate and set out to raise funds for victims of the attacks.

What stands out from these heroic responses is nothing short of collective leadership—not the leader and the led but a community of leaders.

Much of what goes on in schools and organizations, although thankfully not of the order of September 11th is "crisis management." And in times of small or large crises, only those organizations with multiple leaders successfully respond, survive, and become stronger.

High-performing organizations are full of high-performing people. With plentiful opportunities for leadership come plentiful opportunities—nay, demands—for learning on the job. The person who assumes responsibility for something about which he or she cares desperately and whose leadership will influence others in the community stands at the gate of profound learning. For this person also cares desperately to find a way to do it, and to do it well. Thus, a workplace hospitable to widespread leadership will be one hospitable to widespread learning.

And when the workplace is full of both leadership and learning, its inhabitants will flourish and its goals will be reached.

CHAPTER 17

In Place

"**D**ad, we want to have a slumber party. On *Sazerac*."
Joanna and Carolyn, my teenaged daughters, had it all fig-
ured out. They and two friends would plan and procure the food for
dinner and breakfast, organize an evening's entertainment, and
perhaps even sleep a bit aboard *Sazerac* at the Round Pond mooring.
I was invited. This was an offer I wanted to, but couldn't, refuse.

As the early evening mist began to settle in, we rowed out in
Jedediah laden with chips, soda, hamburger, catsup, mustard,
M&Ms, radios, sleeping bags, and jammies. Conspicuous by their
absence were zucchini, beer, cheese, and Oreos.

After a few minutes aboard, it became clear that I had dramatically mixed feelings about being a party to this party. On the one
hand, I wanted to be around to supervise the potentially lethal
propane stove and the marine toilet valves (whose improper use by
recent guests had nearly sunk the vessel), and to keep the hilarity at
a level that would not disturb occupants of neighboring vessels. On
the other hand, I counted five bodies now packed into the cabin, and
four bunks. And I wanted a good nights' sleep.

With the kids' unanimous and enthusiastic approval, I devised a
brilliant plan: one of them would row me to a vacant vessel in the
harbor, of which there were many, and I would surreptitiously spend
the night on a quiet, albeit unfamiliar deck.

After the stove, the valves, and the hilarity had been tended to,
Joanna rowed my air mattress, sleeping bag, poncho, flashlight,

toothbrush, nightshirt, and me into the darkness in search of suitable lodging.

Several criteria for the chosen deck quickly emerged. The winning vessel must be out of earshot of the slumber party, it must have six and one-half feet of unencumbered deck or cockpit, it must be a sailing craft of some distinction and integrity (why not be choosy?), and it must certainly be unoccupied. There was one moral dilemma: I would prefer to ask for permission. But how to ask if no one is aboard? "Better to ask for forgiveness than permission," says my high school principal friend Tom.

As luck would have it, visiting in port that night, a hundred yards abeam of *Sazerac*, lay a beautiful, wooden, forty-eight-foot Tancook whaler. She offered abundant space on the cockpit counter and was clearly dark and vacant. We came alongside the *Zebra Dun* (should her owner ever read these words, I beseech his forgiveness), and the furtive transfer was made. Joanna rowed *Jedediah* back to *Sazerac* where the party now began in earnest. This was a win–win situation if there ever was one.

I slept well in the calm summer air, waking only to cast a couple of sleepy glances over to the slumber party to ensure that it was still afloat, and to catch the distant, muffled giggles rolling gently across the water.

In the first light of early dawn, I checked *Sazerac* again. All was in order. She was on the mooring with dinghy tied astern. The slumberers were slumbering, at last. Then, peering out from beneath my sleeping bag and poncho like the beam from a lighthouse groping through the fog, my eye caught sight of something else. Motion in the harbor. To my horror, a dinghy with three people aboard was just leaving the town dock, and heading straight for the *Zebra Dun*.

I had my opening line ready for the owners when they came alongside: "You may wonder what I'm doing sleeping on your boat." But, unable to think of any subsequent lines, I immediately issued—and obeyed—an order to abandon ship. After glancing wistfully at *Sazerac*'s dinghy many yards away, I took the only remaining option. With heart racing, I quickly stripped to the buff, rolled up my sleeping bag, tossed toothbrush, flashlight, and clothes into the poncho, then lowered these provisions onto the air mattress over the side facing away from the oncoming dinghy.

I slid into the frigid water, which seemed even colder than it had the evening before when my bathing suit had been on. It certainly gave me abrupt notice that *my* slumber party was over. Like a beaver nosing a poplar branch across a pond, I pushed my raft silently toward *Sazerac* with a new respect for the U.S. Navy SEALS.

In the event I should be noticed and intercepted by the oncoming dinghy, I had another opening line ready: "You may wonder what I'm doing stark naked, pushing an air mattress full of stuff across Round Pond at six in the morning." But this time I had some better, less culpable supporting lines. Fortunately, I didn't need any of them. With a mixture of sheer terror, numb relief, and hypothermic shivers, I arrived unobserved alongside *Jedediah*. I began to unload my still-dry gear into the dinghy, just as the other dinghy reached the *Zebra Dun*. Whereupon, to my astonishment, I beheld the occupants row right *past* the Tancook whaler and on to the next vessel, which they boarded, completely unmindful of the little drama that had just unfolded.

Later, over a hot cup of coffee aboard *Sazerac* with the now-wakened slumberers, **Cruising Rule 17** emerged:

 Before you go to great lengths to extricate yourself from trouble, make sure you're in trouble.

~~~~~~~

Last summer, I found myself waiting in an interminable security line at an airport terminal. I was growing impatient, even anxious. My flight departure time was at hand, and the line was barely moving. Suddenly, to my consternation, I discovered that I had left a critical file in my car. It contained the next day's presentation!

Desperately, I said to the woman ahead of me, "I just realized I left something in my car. Would you save my place?"

She nodded. I raced to the parking garage, retrieved the file, ran back to the line, and slipped back into my place. I barely made the flight. Whew!

Shortly after my return from the trip, I delighted in observing some neighborhood youngsters playing Musical Chairs at a birthday party. There was much laughing, pushing and shoving as the music stopped and each child vied for the dwindling seats. And there was much competition and anxiety as well.

As these incidents so vividly suggest, no one likes to lose his or her place. And it's especially difficult to see others in *their* places when we have none.

Sometimes it's fairly clear where or what our place is. "I am an author." Sometimes, though, our place is more ambiguous. When someone asks, "Where do you live?" what do I say? A Boston condo, a trailer in the Keys or on a Maine farm?

At yet other times we have to make choices about place, not knowing ahead of time what the result will be. An adventure, after all, is an experience the outcome of which you do not know in advance!

Will I stay in a secure university position or become an independent consultant? Will I go to the party or stay home and read? Will I push my little raft across Round Pond Harbor or remain in a warm sleeping bag?

And, when choosing, will it be the "right" choice in the long run? What if I make a mistake? What if the circumstances change? What if *I* change and no longer feel "at home" in the place I've chosen? Will I have to change places again? At what cost? When we are without a place in line or a chair we are confused and often frightened. Yet when we do find and commit to a place, we lose some measure of control—also confusing and frightening.

We can take some solace in the words of Mickey Rivers, a sporting philosopher: "Ain't no sense worrying about things you got no control over because if you got no control, ain't no sense worrying. And there ain't no sense worrying about things you got control over, because if you got control, ain't no sense worrying."

Despite this reassurance, there still seems a lot to worry about in our lives. And it often remains difficult to know when we are *in* trouble so that we know when to extricate ourselves *from* trouble.

And so **Working Rule 17:**

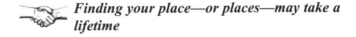 *Finding your place—or places—may take a lifetime*

Wisdom doesn't come from study. Knowledge does. Wisdom comes from the experience of fully showing up for life. Once you commit yourself fully, you may lose a measure of control. But finding your place and committing to it helps define and determine who you are and who you will become.

CHAPTER 18

Inside Passage

A Friendship sloop, although a remarkably accommodating, endearing, and enduring vessel, requires a strong back and an able crew, especially to raise, handle, and reef the huge mainsail. After twenty-two years and three sloops, I no longer had either. I was reminded of a classified ad I had once seen: "Original owner must sell 22' Catboat. Boat in fine condition; owner showing signs of wear." So, with a mixture of great sadness and realism, *Sazerac* was placed into the hands of a caring steward who had both back and crew. Two years later I encountered a very different kind of sailboat, a twenty-six-foot, full-keeled, Contessa sloop.

Mare's Tail is constructed of fiberglass (yes, I know, "If God had intended there to be fiberglass boats, He would have given us fiberglass trees!") and easily stored and maintained in my barn. But her most practical quality is that she is rigged with a roller-furling jib and main and can thus be handily sailed—alone.

Mariners always dream of facing the winds and waves alone. Many have. Joshua Slocum, in 1896, was the first to solo-circumnavigate the globe. And, it turns out, two of the most recent sailors to accomplish this remarkable feat—both the youngest woman and the youngest man—sailed a Contessa.

Whether around the world, around the Horn, or around the bay, there is something profoundly different about sailing single-handed. For, when one goes it alone, he comes up against another relationship—the relationship with himself.

Recently, I sailed from Muscongus Bay to visit a good friend on Isle au Haut, on what became an adventure of a different sort. The first day out offered ample distractions that held my thoughts "out there"—tacking, navigating, dodging pot buoys, preparing and eating meals. Just before nightfall, I picked up a guest mooring off Lookout Point and removed the lifeline which, all day, had kept me safely harnessed to *Mare's Tail*.

Gordie rowed out to greet me in *Wilbur,* his venerable dinghy— a cold beer for me seated on the stern. We enjoyed a fine Isle au Haut dinner complete with hamburgers (his) and zucchini (mine). The next morning, after a good sleep on their guest mooring, I rowed ashore to explore with him the bumpy roads of this raw and remote island. Good truck. Bad roads. Good company. Spectacular island. By noon, with tide falling and wind rising, it was time to return to Muscongus Bay.

Mare's Tail and I romped through Fox Islands Thorofare, across West Penobscot Bay, and into Muscle Ridge Channel. As darkness descended, I anchored for the night in a well-protected little bay behind Whitehead Light. Another day of setting out, reaching out, looking out. Another day, out. After preparing and consuming a modest yet imaginative dinner, prominently featuring zucchini, I slept fitfully.

At daybreak, I opened my eyes. At least I *thought* I opened my eyes. Nothing. I saw nothing. Then I knew: Fog. During the night, an unpredicted thick o' fog had smothered Seal Harbor. I could make out my hand but not the bow. Damn!

My impatience to return home and few provisions aboard suggested setting sail. But perilous currents in the Channel, total obscurity, the Comfort Factor, and perhaps a trace of maturity all dictated sitting tight until this veil of cotton lifted. Having weighed the options, I declared for myself what my young daughters used to call a "jammy day," my first in years. Nowhere to go, nothing to see, nothing to do, and nobody to talk with. A day of enforced relaxation.

My jammy day began with reading, occasionally intruded upon by the sound of a gull or muffled lobster boat engine. For awhile, I read a sea story about a father and son sailing around Cape Horn in a boat *Mare's Tail*'s size. But I was having trouble keeping in mind even this gripping tale. Something was stirring within. I was beginning to feel very uneasy out there in the fog—alone. Seeking the comfort of a familiar voice, I turned on the marine radio for the morning weather report. "Widespread fog. Today and tomorrow." What had begun as a welcome aura of relaxation vanished in the fog. I began to feel trapped . . . with myself.

Like it or not, I guess we are social creatures. A wise theologian reminds us, "Language has created the word *loneliness* to express the pain of being alone and the word *solitude* to express the glory of being alone." For me, solitude had changed to loneliness. I began to talk to myself. Then I invented a companion. To check my position with Loran, I dubbed this navigation instrument "Laura Anne." She gently conversed with me in reassuring numbers. I wished for Snyder, someone, even a slumber party.

Then I heard the powerful engine of a fishing trawler growing louder and closer, it seemed. Despite my radar reflector hanging aloft and certainty that my anchor lay in the mud well away from the Channel and passages into the harbor, a doubting voice began to challenge what I *knew* to be true. I wasn't sure where I was. I began to fear being run over and sunk. I blasted on the foghorn. The sound of the fishing vessel disappeared into the fog. Or had it been there? In my condition of introspection and anxiety, I was experiencing all the benefits of what Outward Bound schools call a "solo."

With growing concern, I began to pay close attention to myself and to what was happening to my slumber party. It was becoming clear in that obscure fog that nothing existed except what was in my head. And what was in my head was not comforting. That discomfort seemed somehow familiar. I recalled being lost in the woods, as a five-year-old. I had haunting thoughts of being left and forgotten at a supermarket.

At this point, I would have given the farm for a brisk northwest wind and unlimited visibility. Yet the demons of the fog continued to torment this solitary skipper. I began preparations for dinner and bedtime—at 2 PM. When nighttime mercifully arrived, I sought safety and comfort in my sleeping bag. I awakened only once to find the stern facing, inexplicably, into the wind. The dream I remembered (or was it a dream?) featured two gigantic lobsters clawing it out on deck until they completely consumed one another. I wondered, had Freud ever gone to sea—alone?

When I awoke in the morning, I immediately peered out the porthole and discerned *land!* A mile visibility. Christopher Columbus could have experienced no greater exhilaration. Within minutes, I was underway. Fog, and my inward-bound experience, soon dissipated as I began, once again, to happily worry about fouling lobster buoys, tide rips, compass headings, and wind directions.

All the way back to Round Pond I contemplated just what kind of companion I am for myself. And, as I thought about my time in the fog confined with myself, I wondered what Cruising Rule might assist a solitary sailor. I had no difficulty appending **Cruising Rule 18:**

 When you cruise alone, be prepared to navigate the "inside passage."

Upon my return to shore, I shared this "off the chart" experience with Mike, my seagoing neighbor down the hill. He once sailed the Pacific, alone, from San Francisco to Hawaii. Mike claims that sailors fall into two camps. Those who, when given time alone, relish it. Away from others, they do whatever they want, whenever they want, however they want. Those in the other camp, he says, dread their own company and can't tolerate themselves for more than an hour. He told of one skipper, racing alone around the world, who found himself so impossible to live with that he radioed ashore: "Abandoned race to save my soul."

The mind of the solo sailor wanders into very peculiar and disturbing places. Mike reported that one night, halfway to Honolulu, he dreamed—he thought it was dream—that a weathered old sailor came aboard, took the helm, and altered course back to California. When Mike awoke, the vessel was on an exact compass course for San Francisco Bay. Another single-hander, when asked if he had experienced any hallucinations, reported, "No, they were all real."

When we are alone, the boundary between reality and illusion becomes very foggy. In the fog, the line becomes even foggier.

In the 1870s the new telegraph was sweeping the country. Henry David Thoreau, informed of a plan to string wires between New England and Texas, questioned, "What in the world could New Englanders and Texans *possibly* have to say to one another?"

A good question. Indeed, what do *any* of us have to say to the rest of us? Sometimes it feels as if the world is so full of endless conversation and chatter that we long for the silence of solitude.

I have a good friend, a bachelor, who has said to me, "You come into this world alone, and you're going to leave this world the same way." He seems to be proud of this fact. At the same time, he is quite a gregarious fellow who stays in touch with many friends and colleagues. One of them once observed, "I think Peter can't stand to be alone with himself. He relies on others to distract him from himself." We may be able to outrun what's outside chasing us, but we cannot outrun what's inside chasing us.

Being alone can have profoundly different meanings. Did we choose it, or was it somehow thrust upon us? How long did it last—too long, not long enough? Was it a respite from the rigors of the workplace, school, or family life? Or banishment? Do we need it periodically to recharge our batteries, or do we gain our energy from being with others? Or both?

Spiritual journeys of isolation and solitude have a remarkable place in the history of many cultures and religions. The New Testament tells of the forty days Jesus spent alone in the desert. The rite of manhood for young Native American boys involved spending several days alone in the forest or prairie. The Buddha reached enlightenment after years of solitary wandering. The capstone of one's Outward Bound adventure is the "solo" in the wilderness.

Going on retreat is a familiar strategy used by organizations and individuals alike to withdraw from everyday work life to reflect, understand, and in some cases, plan for the future. And, sometimes quite unexpectedly, while driving alone in the car or watching the sunrise over Florida Bay, we may have those flashes of insight and understanding that connect us with a deeper meaning.

In all of these experiences we encounter ourselves. But we are social creatures as well, destined to live, love, work, and play with others. Times alone, especially when not sought or wanted, can be austere, even punishing, as I discovered that day in the fog. As we move further away from the community of others, what begins as solitude slowly transforms into loneliness.

For me, the central purpose of my times alone is, above all, to help me understand who I am so that I may better understand my connection with others.

My fog-induced epiphany offers **Working Rule 18:**

 The most critical relationship is the one you have with yourself.

CHAPTER 19

Meetings at Bay

What a great idea! My wife Barbara and I would spend ten days sailing *Mare's Tail,* around Penobscot Bay in August. While in these parts, we would rendezvous with Mike and Kate aboard their new catamaran, *Flying Circus.* Many have set out with similar plans.

Itineraries were shared and cell phone numbers exchanged. Believing with Max Frisch that "Technology is a way of organizing the universe so that man doesn't have to experience it," until recently I swore to throw overboard any cell phone spotted—or heard—aboard my vessel. However, Barbara, my "tech support" in developing entry-level computer skills, presented a compelling brief attesting to the indispensable value of the cell phone for important communications . . . such as meetings at sea. She applied for, demanded, and received a waiver! Thus equipped with all of the electronic marvels of our time—GPS, depth finder, marine radio, and cell phone—we set out.

Upon entering Penobscot Bay before a lovely summer breeze, we decided to put into Pulpit Harbor for the night. We had all agreed to check voicemails and keep our cell phones "open" from 6 to 7 PM. That evening, a message from Mike and Kate reported their intended destination for the following night—Castine, surely Maine's love-liest little seaport village. We called back to confirm—only to read "out of range" on our cell phone. Then, as agreed, we tried the marine radio. Still no connection. We waited in vain for a return call. Oh well, there was still tomorrow.

Barbara and I sailed into Castine the next afternoon, picked up a mooring and prepared for a splendid walk. Leaving the Castine Yacht Club after our first showers in five days, we spotted *Flying Circus* just entering the harbor, a few hundred yards offshore. I hailed Kate, stationed at the bow, and she waved in apparent recognition, whereupon the multihull inexplicably sailed away across Castine Harbor. Oh well, we'd connect later; now that we were within hailing distance, the cell phones would surely work.

When we had satisfied our interest in Castine's historical sites and signs, which revealed that the Dutch, French, English, not to mention Native Americans had quite a history of unfriendly skirmishes at this place, we set out in search of the catamaran and a dinner aboard. We finally spotted *Flying Circus* in Smith Cove. Finding no one aboard, we picked up a nearby mooring, declared it cocktail hour, and waited for Mike and Kate to arrive.

Cocktail hour expired without our friends, so reluctantly we began to ready dinner. Then, we saw them in their inflatable heading our way. Finally! Except they went directly to their transom. As had apparently been the case earlier in the day, despite our array of theatrics, they didn't see us. Only after blowing the decidedly low-tech foghorn did we gain their attention. At last, a *connection*. And a lovely fresh salmon dinner held on a spacious deck that only a catamaran can offer—to which we of course contributed a tired zucchini or two.

So pleased and emboldened were we with our ability to rendezvous at sea that we agreed to connect again for dinner the following night in nearby Holbrook Harbor.

The next afternoon, we sailed to the Penobscot Maritime Museum across the Bay in Searsport. After a tough, uphill slog against wind and current (marred by a salty near-disaster from a galley through-hull valve inadvertently left open), we returned to Holbrook Harbor and picked up a secure mooring. Once again we were delighted to discern Mike and Kate's catamaran two hundred yards away. Unfortunately, it was separated from us by a twenty-five-knot wind on the nose—and by a menacing, invisible obstacle the chart labeled, of all things, "Snyder's Rock."

Although we couldn't paddle our own dinghy—a one-person little kayak—to their boat, we were certain they would see *Mare's Tail*, now visible as a day marker, liberally adorned by drying sleeping bags, mattresses, clothing, and towels fluttering in the rigging.

As time passed with no notice of our presence, we turned once again to that miracle of communication, the cell phone. We attempted to call Mike and Kate, only to be greeted by obscure, garbled voice messages. As daylight waned and the winds waxed, we tried the searchlight, then the ship-to-shore radio. Then we dined—by ourselves.

The next day Barbara and I walked some lovely paths in the Holbrook Island Sanctuary. While devouring our little lunch at a sandy cove, who should pass by, a few hundred yards offshore, heading south, but Mike and Kate and *Flying Circus,* once again so close and yet so oblivious to our presence. We watched them pass. Clearly, fate had set another course for us all—the one we were on, not the one we had planned.

When we finally caught up with Kate and Mike, back at home, **Cruising Rule 19** was launched:

 Ships can pass in the day—as well as the night!

What a great idea! The dean had asked me to direct a study on the Harvard Graduate School of Education and Schools. The year was 1979. The task, to look carefully and critically at ways the school was—and was not—involved with schooling in the United States, write a report outlining the current state of affairs, and make recommendations for the future. It was an important effort and a vote of high confidence bestowed upon a public school principal, early in his career.

The stakes were high. Recommendations from this study promised to affect profoundly the future course and curriculum of the school. Additionally, the university's president had promised to fund two new faculty positions at the school if the Harvard community accepted the report and its recommendations.

I set to work. I spent several weeks planning the project—what reports I would read, who I would interview, with whom I would consult, what other schools of education I would visit, and how I might frame the report. Ambitious, hopeful plans.

Then I set about interviewing alumni across the country, students in master's and doctoral programs, members of the faculty, the dean, and the president. What did each see going on at the intersection between the School of Education and schools? What would each like to see? I read about school–university relationships in other places. Then I visited the most intriguing, noting promising practices. The data sources may not have been completely exhausted, but I was!

Difficult as it was, the planning part of the effort was nothing compared with what lay ahead. After six months, the data collecting was completed, and it was time to craft the report and attempt to shepherd it through the mazes of academia.

The conclusions I had reached were bleak. I found (and wrote) that "the School has become dangerously aloof from the business about which it purports to teach and do research . . . schooling." For financial, political and other reasons, the school had recently abolished programs in teacher and administrative preparation, curriculum, guidance, and other areas that lie at the very heart of the mission of most schools of education. Left were many programs in areas such as the economics of education, international education, sociology, and history of education. Faculty members whose programs had been eliminated were outraged, as were alumni, most of whom work in schools. "Was this a school of education or a school of social science?" many demanded to know.

A committee of eight senior faculty members, plus the dean, was responsible for overseeing me and for reviewing and signing off on the Report—or not. I showed each the first draft. Because it was highly critical of the direction the school was taking, many of them became outraged at what they saw as a biased and unfair portrait.

Woodrow Wilson, when he vacated his position as president of Princeton University to become governor of New Jersey, was asked why he was making the change. "I can't stand the politics," he said.

I soon began to learn *my* lessons about academic politics. A major reason I had been enlisted to write the report was that I was a public school practitioner and an alumnus of the school with demonstrated writing capability. My experience and allegiance *was* decidedly tilted toward helping schools and school people. Now, writing a report critical of the School of Education, I soon lost my hold on what fragile first-class citizenship I might have enjoyed within the

University. A vote of no confidence by the faculty committe loomed large.

At about this time I remember following the lead of Dean Acheson and placing on my desk three baskets:

IN

OUT

TOO HARD

The situation demanded a new strategy: to visit the senior faculty members again and find out exactly what each objected to in the report. Then, with their help and cooperation, I hoped to rework the objectionable sections and add others about which they felt strongly. Many responded in helpful ways. Unfortunately, there was much disagreement within the faculty; what offended one pleased another. And there was much disagreement about the state of the school. All the while I was in the middle, feeling like a boat fender between a dock and a pitching vessel in a nor'easter.

I spent many more weeks running this academic gauntlet of massive intellects and formidable egos, sometimes sitting stoically for a severe reprimand, sometimes holding my ground and pushing back; sometimes holding hands, sometimes smoothing ruffled feathers, sometimes having my own feathers ruffled . . . and oftentimes longing to be back in my elementary school!

It was a highly iterative process. When I had just about succeeded in revising a document that could enlist eight signatures plus the dean's, another important figure would weigh in with outrage that he or she had not been consulted or had been misunderstood or misrepresented. Then revisions would begin anew. Draft upon draft. And at the eleventh hour, yet another draft.

As I was reeling on the ropes, desperately needed and welcome editorial assistance and political cover emerged from some of the senior faculty members, who threw their considerable weight behind the project. Finally, mercifully, the eight signatures were gained, and with them, the dean's support.

But even this was just the beginning. Next the report went to the entire faculty of the School of Education, some eighty-five strong, many of whom I had not consulted to this point.

Then to members of the Alumni Council, many of whom objected that the report had been "watered down." Another gauntlet to run.

And finally to the president of Harvard for his sanction.

Learning that people, too, can pass in the day as well as the night, I became a convert to **Working Rule 19:**

 *Planning is hard; execution is harder.*

Somehow—and I'm still not sure how—the Report on the Harvard Graduate School of Education and Schools was accepted and ratified. Two new faculty positions at the school were funded by the President's Office, $100,000 was raised to begin implementing the recommendations of the report. The first order of business was to create a Principals Center, of which I became the director.

Reading this story is perhaps as taxing for you as living it was for me. And possibly as taxing as your own experiences in planning and execution. We spend enormous amounts of time developing and refining plans. Some even hold full-time positions as planners. But no matter how exhaustively we plan, it's difficult to foresee all the complexities and contingencies inherent in execution—the wind on our nose, the computer network crashing, and the unknown colleagues whose support must be gained. We must anticipate the unknown, the unforeseen, and the unwanted. Cell phones are not enough.

CHAPTER 20

Skinflint Skippers

"How much did it cost?" the guest inquired, admiring J. P. Morgan's three-hundred-foot yacht, *Corsair.*

"If you have to ask, you can't afford one," replied Mr. Morgan.

Countless others have since pondered the connection between boats and dollars.

Ever since we met at age fifteen, Gordon and I have been friendly competitors—beginning with our Model A Fords. Whose was in best shape? Whose restoration was superior? Whose classic automobile was most attractive to the girl with whom we were both infatuated?

In more recent times, Gordon has taken up sailing. In but a few years his vessels jumped from sixteen feet to twenty-six-feet to thirty feet. He was a goner. Quite naturally, Gordon and I began to compete about sailing. Not, as one might suppose, in boat length, speed, class, or even beauty. You see, Gordon, married to a Scottish lass, is a very frugal person. I am a parsimonious Yankee. It was only natural that our competition in boats would have to do with money. Our continuing midlife duel is not over who spends the *most* but who spends the *least* on his insatiable sailing habit.

Our calculations are not based simply upon annual yard bills, insurance premiums, or new equipment. Gordon, a shrewd business-man, insists that the only proper standard for competing is determined by who, at the end of the sailing season, enjoys the most favorable cost-per-sailing-day ratio. Theoretically, one could emerge from a sailing season with each day spent aboard costing ten dollars—say, a $3,300 total expense for 330 sailing days. Theoretically.

In our attempt to minimize The Ratio (and rationalize this expensive habit), we agreed to count days spent aboard even when we never got off the mooring (sleeping aboard to break the July heat spell, for instance) and to count the days our children spent on the boat without us (their night on the town, for instance). We also counted any fragment of a day spent on the boat (driving out to check the automatic bilge pump, for instance).

But ever-increasing costs wreak havoc on tight-fisted Scots and Yankee skippers. For years Gordon and I bantered about The Ratio. We especially enjoyed taunting each other when one of us came aboard to share a sail—thereby reducing the host's cost/sail ratio while the guest was held captive, unable to do the same. Of course, a two- or three-day cruise worked best of all to cause one's penurious companion to suffer.

I knew The Ratio was getting out of hand when I realized one day, with a fresh breeze up, that I couldn't enjoy working in the garden or tending my bees. I should be out sailing. Nor was I much looking forward to sailing that summer with Gordon on his boat because of the damage this would inflict on my competitive advantage.

Only once, after hauling for the year, did Gordon and I actually compute our "per unit cost." After carefully considering, and attempting to minimize, all "sailing-related costs" (Must the new roof rack on the car for the dinghy count? After all, it's often used for the bicycle), we each plugged our figures into the calculator, along with our days aboard, documented in the log.

Unfortunately, that particular season for me had been rainy, foggy, and windless, with a major expenditure on a new rudderpost. After due deliberation, and having withstood each other's demands for an "audit," Gordon's cost-per-day of sailing came out to $510; mine was $570. He won.

But we both lost, because this exercise put a chill on our sailing habits like a cold, October northwesterly. We never repeated it. For we learned **Cruising Rule 20:**

 If you have to ask how much it costs, you'll never be able to enjoy it.

Gordon and I continue to taunt one another about The Ratio. But we have resolved that our experiences sailing must be assessed by means other than money: New learning about seamanship, navigation, self; unforgettable adventures, friendships made and deepened, and new waters explored. Never again will we reduce that which provides nourishment for the soul to dollars and cents. For if we calculate the cost of what we enjoy most in life, we will no longer enjoy it.

~~~~~~~~~

Ratios are useful. They help us measure the tangible and the intangible in life: miles per hour, parts per million, dollars per hour, widgets per day, percent answers correct on a test. And dollars cost per sailing day! At work, at school and at home, we depend on ratios to give meaning to endless pieces of disordered information. They help us monitor our lives and make important decisions. "I'm not getting my money's worth." "This isn't worth the effort."

The business world relies on ratios to measure the success (or failure) of an enterprise. Price earnings ratios. Return on investment. Percent market share. Dollars per share of stock. The business section of the paper is full of little graphs measuring various ratios, important to someone. These reams of ratios enable us to put a stake in the ground; they provide a reference point, which informs our day to day behavior.

But, while useful, ratios are also tricky. How do you decide what to put on the top and the bottom? What if you have more than two or three things you want to compare simultaneously? And what happens when the usefulness of the ratio doesn't endure?

While students struggle to pass state standardized tests and meet higher and higher standards to obtain a high school diploma, an increasing number of colleges and universities have decided to no longer require SAT scores as part of the admissions process. Without these dominating "objective" measures of intelligence, they now choose to attend to perhaps more important subjective measures of worth like character, creativity and service.

A colleague of mine has been studying high school valedictorians, looking at their performance in life, subsequent to graduation. He is discovering that valedictorians perform less well in later life by many measures than do those who ranked below them in high school. For instance, they are underrepresented in the professions such as law, academia, and medicine. Correct answers per exam may not be as powerful a ratio as we suppose.

Ratios may tell us little about value. The value of doing business in our capitalistic society is measured by what we might gain—usually called profit. But, although value is related to money, it is not the same. There are times when we must assign quality of effort and time in less concrete units.

Consider all the varieties of relationships in which we participate: professional, personal, casual, profound, episodic, lifelong. Our associations with others have high value. And they bring costs. Among the costs I have experienced are the time relationships consume, dealing with conflict, sharing decisions. And the restrictions they place on my ability to make unilateral decisions quickly. Relationships demand that I be selfless, not selfish; caring rather than carefree.

But, like a boat, if you have to ask how much a relationship costs, you'll probably never be able to enjoy it. I find it far more useful and conducive to satisfying relationships to focus not on costs but on value. Who can say what a relationship is worth? Associated with quality are so many intangibles: learning, trust, acceptance, humor, adventure, respect, sacrifice. Here, the spreadsheet of the workplace offers little assistance.

For me the value in a good relationship comes in many forms: companionship in times of celebration, help in times of need, company in times of loneliness, affirmation in times of doubt. And, every bit as much, value in relationships comes in the reward I experience contributing to and participating in the life of another. We make a living by what we get; we make a life by what we give.

Relationships bring value, which cannot—and must not—be measured by common means. If we attempt to calculate "the ratio," the costs per relationship day, we risk no longer *having* a relationship. Brian Weiss tells us, "We are here to learn and to love. Nothing else really matters."

Working Rule 20 about relationships is akin to what we've said about boats:

 If you have to ask how much it costs, you may never value it.

CHAPTER 21

Both Feet In

Embarking on a cruise, or even a day sail, is an exciting and complex event. Details are crucial: provisions, flotation devices, charts, sleeping bags, zucchini. And timing. If the captain pronounces that the vessel will depart at 10 AM, guests should arrive at the dock well beforehand. Occasionally, the captain may arrive first, but under no circumstances must he ever have to wait for a guest's late arrival. Missing the tide or wasting a wind makes the captain cranky.

But having to be on time at the beginning of a cruise is less important than not having to be on time at the end. No guest should ever come aboard with impending commitments ashore. While at sea, safety, navigation, and sailing the wind, not the obligations of the guests, must be the captain's priorities. When the concerns of guests are put before the laws of nature, a price will be paid.

Ask Reverend Fred. As a guest on *Sazerac* one weekend, he insisted on being back ashore to greet his flock by 11 AM one Sunday morning. Before the sun had risen, we had to vacate a perfectly safe anchorage on an offshore island, set out into a gale, and sail double-reefed through eight-foot seas across Muscongus Bay to get back to the mainland. The dinghy capsized, we lost the oars, fractured the gaff (again), and we had to tie the pastor into the cockpit with docking lines, as green water broke over the cabin house and the clergyman. Periodically, the good reverend lost his lunch over the side. Several times we nearly lost him. Reverend Fred still contends that he prayed all the way across and would, in the time-honored tradition, have promised God to build Him a church, if safely delivered, had they not already had a perfectly good one in Portland.

Upon setting foot on land, the vicar—ashen, soaking wet, dehydrated, nauseated, but grateful for my part in his safe deliverance—removed his handsome, dripping bowtie, in which he had left the island clad for worship, and presented it to me in somber supplication. It still adorns my closet door. And every time I see it, it reminds me of **Cruising Rule 21:**

 Never let anyone on board who has to get off board—for God's sake!

The service commenced at 11 AM sharp, with Reverend Fred at the helm. The parishioners are still talking about it.

A student at Harvard was once asked, "Is the biggest problem at your university ignorance or apathy?"

Whereupon the student replied, without hesitation, "I don't know and I don't care!"

The story is, I hope, apocryphal. But not the sentiment. How many of us have worked in the company of others who convey in multiple languages, "I don't care."

"Only two years until I retire!"

"TGIF!"

The colleague who works on another task during the project meeting.

And that teacher who comes to the faculty meeting with overcoat on, ready to go home.

The presence of others with one foot out the door is corrosive to one's spirit—to the culture of the workplace and to the work to be done.

What brings out the best in us most of the time is a work culture characterized not by half-hearted passivity but by full-hearted, passionate *commitment.* Not one foot out the door but two feet *in* the door. Buy-in, it's often called. All of us want to work in a place where our colleagues believe in and are committed to their work. Indeed, *we* want to believe in and be committed to what *we* are doing. We respect ourselves, others and the important work to be done when all are deeply committed to being there and to doing it.

Perhaps you have heard the story about two businessmen having breakfast one morning and discussing commitment. "You see those eggs?" asked one. "Those chickens *participated* in our meal. But look at the bacon. That hog was *committed* to our breakfast!"

Commitment is a promise, a pledge, to do or be something. It is the unqualified pursuit of a goal, even in the face of reservations and obstacles. We commit to something or someone—to chair a committee, to be a teacher, to marry a loved one—because we feel it is the right thing to do.

Transforming vision into reality will never come from merely putting in time. Participating is necessary but not sufficient. Showing up is *not* 85 percent of life, Woody Allen notwithstanding. At least not when there is important work to be done. "To commit" is an active not a passive verb. It's what you do, not just what you feel. We achieve our goals only through active individual and collective commitment to them.

To commit also means to sustain the effort—whether in the face of eight-foot seas or uncertain resources. So before you start, make sure you will finish.

Former Princeton basketball coach Pete Carril puts it this way in **Working Rule 21:**

 To achieve excellence one must want to become good enough bad enough.

I heard a story about a kindergarten child asked to draw a picture of an important figure in her life. With her crayons, she was carefully limning a highly unusual picture which drew the attention of her puzzled teacher.

Teacher: "What are you drawing?"

Child: "God."

Teacher: "But no one knows what God looks like."

Child: "They will when I'm done."

All of us can learn a great deal about commitment from the innocence, creativity, and confidence displayed by this five-year-old. It's about having a goal, believing in the goal, and faithfully sustaining commitment to achieving the goal—especially in the face of many doubts and doubters.

CHAPTER 22

Promises, Promises

The parable of Reverend Fred and the troubled waters suggests that the return from a sail is a matter of considerable consequence. If the necessity for an early return dampens the relationships among those aboard ship, the necessity of a late return places the relationships between those aboard and others waiting ashore in peril.

Our complicated culture places many obligations upon us which pile up, mercilessly, one upon the other. We run breathlessly from one commitment to the next, but somehow it works—most of the time.

I used to set out to sea promising to return for a PTA meeting at 8 PM, a game at Fenway Park at 7 PM, or, heaven forbid, a flight to Cincinnati at 6 PM. "I'll be there!" Sure.

I assembled a powerful armada of truthful and compelling excuses for being late, which, over the years, demolished many a bridge spanning my life at sea with those waiting ashore:

Tide came in and stole dinghy from the beach

Went aground

Failure of rigging

Hadn't finished Long Version

Took longer than expected to apply cat's-ass brindle

Good fishing

Prop hopelessly fouled in lobster buoy

Becalmed, engine wouldn't start

Just becalmed

Forgot the Comfort Factor

Unexpected wind shift

Had to improve The Ratio

Couldn't get off mooring; couldn't get mooring off

Couldn't decide who I was and what to wear

Fog

The Town Fathers . . .

These excuses, no matter how honestly tendered, wore danger-ously thin with time, like the threadbare heel of an overused sock. No one ashore seemed to share my amusement in all of this, let alone to understand.

The truth of the matter is that when you get on, even near, a sail-boat, you can't anticipate what is going to happen. Each voyage brings a different surprise. Therefore, it is both impossible and unwise to commit to when you will return.

Hence the absolute necessity for **Cruising Rule 22:**

 When you go to sea, don't promise to return— especially at an agreed-upon time.

I have subsequently found it useful, if somewhat redundant ("Like using a belt and suspenders," Snyder says), to employ the fol-lowing algebraic formula, and instruct those ashore in its applica-tion, as an aid for calculating my *actual* time of return:

$$x = 2n + 1,$$

where x = the actual number of hours until return and n = the number of hours until promised return.

Or, if I say I shall be back from the boat in four hours, double that (eight) and add an hour for good measure. Hence, expect me in nine hours.

With few promises made, and with the addition of the above "nautical aid," these days there are few time violations, few hard feelings, and little need for explanations.

P romises, promises.
   "I'll have the car home by 4 so you can get to your doctor's appointment at 5." The car, and apologetic driver, arrive—at 5:15.

In the previous chapter, we considered the nature of commitments and the importance in our lives of having them. But what happens when we have difficulty making *good* on our commitments?

To be seen as unreliable—to *be* unreliable—is a condition not long tolerated in a relationship. Only one thing is more toxic and destructive than a promise made and not kept: a *pattern* of promises made and not kept.

This is every bit as true in the workplace as it is in personal relationships. A work culture where commitments are made:

"You'll manage the next project."

"We'll use everybody's input."

"You'll be getting a bonus."

and violated:

"Sorry, Sally is going to manage the project."

"Management has decided to . . . ."

"Sorry, no bonus this year."

is not a culture hospitable to a fulfilling work life or one capable of eliciting anyone's best efforts? Violation of promises erodes the fundamental basis for trust in any relationship.

I'm reminded of a fourth-grade teacher we once hired. To our dismay, we soon discovered that this teacher had severe difficulties being on time. The mornings when the teacher arrived well after his students telegraphed alarming messages to students, colleagues, and me.

I heard youngsters saying:

"He doesn't like us."

"Is he OK?"

And teachers saying:

"He doesn't really want to be teaching here."

"He needs help with his time management skills."

And I heard myself asking:

"Is his personal life out of control?"

"Is he challenging authority, daring me to call him on his behavior?"

"Did we make a mistake in hiring him?"

A number of different responses, each calling into question the teacher's ability as well as his intentions to fulfill his professional responsibilities.

So accustomed were all of us in the school to meeting our obligations in a timely manner and so serious were the consequences on the lives of children if we didn't, that the act of showing up late for class a few times quickly generated serious concerns about this teacher. All of them jeopardized his entry and his future success in the new setting.

Among the excuses he brought with him—belatedly—were:

"I underestimated how long it would take to get here."

"I had to depend on the bus. It was late."

"I didn't think the kids came in from the playground until later."

So what was the principal going to do about this teacher's growing pattern of tardiness? I remember engaging in different responses, in an ascending order of magnitude:

INCIDENT 1: CONCERN

"Is everything all right at home? Are you OK? Is there anything I can do to help?"

INCIDENT 2 (TWO WEEKS LATER): WORRY

"This is the second time this month this has happened."

"I'm worried about the youngsters being left unattended."

"It was unfair for me to walk out on a parent conference to cover your class. The parents were alarmed."

INCIDENT 3 (A WEEK LATER): EXASPERATION

"Is this the way you do life?"

"This can't happen again. We've got to work out a solution so it doesn't. Call me if you know you are going to be late."

INCIDENT 4 (A FEW DAYS LATER, WHEN HE CALLS ANOTHER TEACHER TO COVER HIS CLASS, AND TRIES TO SNEAK IN FROM THE PARKING LOT, 15 MINUTES LATE): ANGER, THREATS OF SANCTIONS

"If you are going to teach here, you *must* make good on your commitment to show up on time."

"The next time you are late, I will file a written reprimand in your permanent folder."

INCIDENT 5 (A WEEK LATER): SANCTIONS

Written reprimand in the folder.

Beginning of documentation for possible dismissal.

Three-way conference with assistant superintendent for personnel.

And so it went. Consequences for showing up late clearly had a huge influence on this teacher's career. And on his pupils. But it also exacted a price on other teachers. One teacher, when asked for help by her breathless, errant colleague, uttered in exasperation, "Lack of planning on *your* part does not constitute an emergency on *my* part!"

After repeated and unsuccessful attempts—by him and by me—to remedy the problem, I reluctantly let him go.

He was a fine teacher. What I thought we were getting when we hired him, we got. A fine teacher. But with him also came an inability to be on time, to make good on his commitment to his colleagues, his students, and his profession.

Our relationships with one another suffer terribly, often irreparably when commitments are not met. Reactions to a pattern of broken promises clearly progress from concern, through annoyance, inconvenience, then anger, and inexorably toward termination of the relationship.

And in most work settings, the few who violate their agreements often cause restrictive policies to be constructed which affect all. And of course the strictures crafted for the few insult, infantilize, and demoralize the many. They often have more negative influence on the innocent than positive influence on the guilty.

All the more essential to have and to attend to **Working Rule 22:**

 *Underpromise and overdeliver.*

A promise to be on time, like most of our commitments, is made with every intention of fulfilling it. Few deliberately set out to deceive, disappoint or betray those around them. We promise because we believe that we'll come through and we want to. We are mystified that those, like the tardy teacher, who are repeatedly guilty of breaking their promises, seem oblivious to their deviant patterns and incapable of addressing them. Yet like me, the habitual late sailor, we all prove gifted and talented at shamelessly employing every outrageous excuse under the sun—from "the tide came in and stole the dinghy from the beach" to "I didn't think the kids came in from the playground until later."

A trail of broken promises is inevitably accompanied by a trail of broken relationships. Conversely, there is no more powerful bond in strengthening a relationship than complying fully with what you have led others to expect of you. Even better, delivering *more* than you have led them to expect.

Hence the absolute necessity for we who have trouble making good on our promises to devise some crutches which can carry our enfeebled efforts. For those of you who have trouble with making good on *your* promises, alas, I have no silver bullet or magic potion. I can only commend to you $x = 2n + 1$.

CHAPTER 23

Fair Winds

In Maine, there are two seasons: winter and August. The annual Columbus Day boys' night on the town notwithstanding, four months is about all a skipper can squeeze out of the New England sailing summer— one third of the year. Yet I know of no sailor ready to swallow the anchor and hang up his passion the other two thirds. Not me. So I have taken a tip from the noble osprey and now live a migratory life. Barbara and I flee to warmer climates for the winter. At twenty-five degrees latitude, southern waters remain in their liquid state, and sailing can continue.

A few years ago, I found, along the shores of Florida Bay, a hundred-dollar dwelling on a million-dollar site. Here, an hour and a half from Miami, we enjoy complete solitude in one of the least known and most extraordinary sailing grounds in the world—850 wet, square miles of the Everglades National Park.

Our winter sloop is a gaff-rigged, seventeen-foot catboat. Although its origins are in Cape Cod, it is made for these waters. For in the winter, the winds and bottom are soft, the waters are blue and warm, and the manatee and dolphin are more common than harbor seals in Muscongus Bay. The feeling of exhilaration we experience aboard a graceful sailing vessel breezing across the water on a beam reach, while osprey and gulls wheel and screech overhead, reminds us of summer along the Maine coast.

A sailing vessel is capable of two forms of locomotion: sailing and motoring (not counting drifting a mooring across a harbor or being trucked to the barn in the fall). A proper sailing vessel always sails.

For many years I believed that "For the sailor without a destination there is no favorable wind; for the sailor with a destination, every wind is favorable." Until recently.

Bob, a very orderly sort, called to invite our friend Jack and me to help move his sailboat from a dock in Key Largo to a new berth on Plantation Key. The plan was to sail the following week down the narrow Intracoastal Waterway in a southwesterly direction. No problem. Almost any wind would get us there—except southwesterly. (Sailboats are great, but their only drawback is an inability to sail directly into the wind—especially into a lot of it.) Prevailing winds during most of the winter in the Florida Keys are east-southeast and north during the occasional cold fronts. Never southwest.

When I awoke on the appointed Sunday, my little weather station reported the bad news: a wind direction of 225 degrees—due southwest. Worse news was the anemometer spinning madly at twenty-five to thirty-five knots. The good news? No mosquitoes.

That day brought the strongest and most unrelenting southwesterlies anyone could remember. We boys were forced to motor all the way, under small-craft warnings, getting hammered on the nose for five salty, wet, lumpy hours. The day reminded me of the name I once saw emblazoned on a transom: *Passing Wind.*

The day following our trip, the winds blew favorably from the north, as the day before the trip they had blown favorably from the east. There could be only one possible explanation.

Apparently, the mysterious work of the Town Fathers respects no boundaries. These devils, in their whimsy, rearrange not only navigation aids along the Maine coast but winds along Florida Bay. Clearly, the sailor with a carefully planned destination lives at the mercy of the Town Fathers; the sailor who does not have, or does not disclose, a planned course cannot be confounded by the capricious winds—or Fathers. He confounds Them. Hence, **Cruising Rule 23:**

When you declare your intention to sail in a particular direction, the winds will come strong from that direction.

Sailing is an activity best undertaken when you have no need to get anywhere in particular. Bob, Jack, and I agreed that hence forth, when we *must* sail to a specific destination, we will call the others late the night before, at the last moment, when the Town Fathers are abed, and whisper ever so quietly into the phone, "I'm thinking possibly about maybe sailing to Islamorada. Want to come along?"

～～～～～～～

"Whatever can go wrong, will go wrong." I've never met Mr. Murphy, but I am certain that he was a seafaring fellow. And I'm equally sure that he had extensive experience in the workplace.

Who hasn't walked in his shoes? At one time or another each of us has developed a soaring vision for a new product or school, transformed it into concrete goals and then devised an exquisite plan, certain to lead to our new destination. All the while we have involved others in the process. Then—life happens. Obstacles, impediments, problems, obstructers, and naysayers suddenly proliferate and swarm like fruit flies around an aging melon.

Despite our best intentions, well-made plans and an impeccable democratic process, winds turn, inexplicably, onto our nose. We are surprised, perplexed, angered, frustrated, and discouraged by our inability to move forward. Even if the merit of the effort is intuitively obvious to an idiot!

I've seen grown men and women in tears when their unassailable plans were assailed. I've seen *myself* in tears. So what are we to do with this recurring predicament in our work? We are hired and paid to produce. How do you do that? Murphy's Law may be inevitable and immutable, but our response to it need not be.

Over the years, I have found myself pursuing a variety of options—with varying degrees of success:

1. MANIPULATE

Diplomacy has been defined as the art of allowing someone else to have your way. We have all experienced attempts by others to manipulate us. We find out that the stated purpose of a project, although somewhat true, was in fact a cover for management's real purpose. We realize we've been "had."

As P. T. Barnum put it, "You can fool most of the people some of the time . . . and usually that's sufficient." But not in the workplace. Our manipulations are uncovered and smoked out. The inevitable feedback is predictably brutal: "come clean," "disclose," "be up front." If we are the manipulator, not the manipulatee, we are in for some richly deserved anger from those who feel betrayed. Most likely, unless we are very skillful or very powerful, we will experience loss of trust and cooperation from our colleagues.

2. WITHHOLD

Protect your plan with all the secrecy of a military invasion. Disclose only portions of your intentions, just enough to be able to say, "I told you at the meeting last month." Then wait until the very last minute to spring the full plan. The naysayers will not have time to mobilize and to subvert. Act suddenly, decisively and with finality in implementing the plan.

Waiting until the eleventh hour may indeed ward off initial obstruction. But then, as we find out, after that brilliant presentation to staff, they return to their cubicles, turn to the wall and continue as before.

3. DENY

We have all heard of four-letter words. As principal I used to hear, in response to any fresh, new exciting idea that emanated from me—or from anyone else—an equally objectionable four-word sentence. "They'll never let us." I never knew who "they" were, but it was commonly believed that as soon as we tried cross-age grouping or revised our pupil evaluation system from letter grades to written comments, "they" would spring from behind a bush and nullify attempts to fulfill our dreams. So I denied that opposition existed. "Paper tigers," I used to assure the faculty.

Until I was fired. Sometimes "they" are undeniably real tigers!

4. POWER UP

If, I reasoned, I could develop a repertoire of ways of powering through the opposition, then new ideas and plans would fly. If there is too much wind on the nose, use the engine. If there is *no* wind or engine, power up with oars.

Employ carrots that generate buy-in—incentives of pay, career advancement, and that corner office. And employ sticks that stifle opposition—a negative performance appraisal, sitting on a request for transfer, a low-end merit raise.

I found that the more I attempted to "power up," the more likely my plans would be sabotaged. Furthermore, I learned that reliance on power often fosters a culture of fear, superficial compliance, and passive resistance. "This too shall pass."

5. ADJUST

The lifeblood of any organization—and any relationship—is knowing when and how to adjust.

On the job, when the contract bid is accepted on Tuesday and then precipitously rejected on Thursday, adjust. There are a number of ways I've found to adjust to sudden violation of hope and opposition to plans.

Don't Do It . . . Now

Why did Bob and Jack and I spend a full day motoring into high winds, drenched with stinging salt spray, when the following days were likely to offer a favorable breeze? Because we planned it and wrote it in our calendars a month ago. We were committed! So why, in the face of known, severe conditions, didn't we stay home that day and read the Sunday *Times*?

Have Options

Go in to Plan A with Plans B and C on the ready. If a running game is being thwarted, employ a passing game. Plan ahead for contingencies of failure. When your horse is dead, dismount! Have another saddled up, ready to go.

Together, Reinvent on the Spot

Success is not final; failure is not fatal. Resist the temptation to circle a wagon and go it alone. Ask for help. In the face of now-known impediments and new information, invite others to reflect together, brainstorm together, and invent together a more promising way. I now try to be open to the possibility of human error in myself—and equally open to the possibility of human wisdom in others.

A principal in Michigan once lamented to me, "It isn't the height of the mountains that wears me down, it's the pebbles in my shoes." All too often we are the pebbles in other's shoes–and in our own shoes–and our primitive skills in workplace relationships are insufficient to shake them out.

So let's keep in mind **Working Rule 23:**

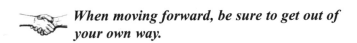 *When moving forward, be sure to get out of your own way.*

The superior sailor possessing superior knowledge uses his superior knowledge to stay out of situations in which he will not have to *use* his superior knowledge.

I have found that many of the major problems we face in our work are the result of a discrepancy between the way humans think and the way human nature works. And I remind myself that difficult obstacles are placed in our way not to stop us, but to summon our courage, our strength, our intelligence and our resolve.

CHAPTER 24

Can You Help Me?

Cruising Florida Bay in our little catboat is one of Barbara's and my favorite pastimes. This triangle of skinny water between the mainland of South Florida and the Upper Keys is the southernmost border of the Everglades National Park and home to an astonishing assortment of life. "Wild Kingdom," we call it.

The "backcountry," as it's known to the locals, is like no other place; quiet, mysterious, and dotted with uninhabited mangrove islands with names like Calusa, Buttonwood, Black Betsy, and Bob Allen. Also known as keys, these tangles of roots, mud, and leaves seem to float just above the endless horizon. The shallow waters, rarely more than six feet deep and usually much less, turn from azure to green to sandy brown to chocolate, depending on sunlight, clouds, seagrass, mudbanks—and depth. Narrow, winding channels, like Twisty Mile, Tin Can Alley, and Crocodile Dragover, lead safely over the flats and basins. Even a boat like ours, drawing only twenty-three inches—knee deep—can easily go aground in the soft, sticky marl. Osprey, white pelicans, tarpon, and manatee are here in abundance. But, blessedly, the only human presence is the occasional flats fisherman. It is a liquid wilderness, right in our backyard.

Last winter, we set out into the backcountry for a long weekend. On the last leg of our journey, we decided to head for Manatee Key, where a lovely little protected cove offers safe anchorage for the night. It would be a short trip home the next day.

Manatee Key is surrounded by a mudbank that can be traversed only through a disturbingly shallow, narrow channel. We found and carefully navigated "Manatee Cut," scarcely wider than the beam of our boat and marked obscurely by what looked like a couple of inverted hockey sticks rising ten feet out of the mud.

We dropped anchor in the cove, ate supper, and settled in for the evening. Two roseate spoonbills, the most beautiful and rare of Everglades birds, circled overhead, their rich pink color deepened by the setting sun reflecting off their wings. We were in Paradise—and knew it.

We awoke abruptly about 3 AM. Something had changed. The evening breeze had vanished. It was oppressively hot, humid, and still in the predawn darkness. The tropical air in the small cabin was heavy and close. What was worse, a thick cloud of buzzing insects had penetrated the mosquito netting, and was feasting on our flesh. Paradise had vanished. No light, no air, no sleep, no-see-ums!

"Let's get the hell out of here!" exclaimed this well-bitten sailor.

"I totally agree," replied Barbara. "But we'll have to figure out how to find our way back to Manatee Cut in the dark. We barely made it in broad daylight."

With some sense of urgency and haste we surveyed the situation and took inventory of our resources. There was faint starlight but no moon. We had a flashlight, compass, chart, and an unreliable outboard motor. And we vaguely remembered the landscape of water and mud from the day before.

"If I lay a compass course for the Cut, can you read the water depth and look for the markers?" I asked.

"Yup. I'll take the flashlight to the bow and sweep down and out. I'll do my best to see the bottom, but will you be ready to jump over and push us off if we go up on a mudbank?"

"I'll push off if you can maneuver the outboard in reverse."

"Haven't done that before, but you can coach me."

Desperately in need of one another's help to pull this off, we engaged in some highly motivated "on-the-job training." Or else we would spend the rest of the night feeding a new bunch of blood-thirsty critters.

With outboard purring hopefully, we set out, ever vigilant for the slow, sticky halt that would indicate we had grounded on mud.

After five interminable minutes and a trail of muddy water behind us—hallelujah! Barbara's good nighttime eyes spotted the elusive poles. After successfully threading this oozy needle, we turned the boat, quietly, and with relief into deeper water, and headed into the dawn for home.

The sky exploded into a rosy coral that deepened as the sun appeared—almost the same color as the roseate spoonbills we'd seen the evening before, as if to announce **Cruising Rule 24:**

 When in the thick of it, go through the thin of it.

"**C**an you help me?"

Frequently in our work lives we get asked for help from our colleagues. And less often (to be sure!), we find ourselves in the position of needing *their* help. The ability to offer help when asked and to ask for help when needed denotes a strong and healthy work culture. Just as on a boat—or in a relationship—part of being a good companion is being able to ask for and accept help from one another.

Requests for help can range from the mundane ("Can you watch my phones while I go to lunch?") to the unusual ("I know it's 3 AM, but can we get going?") or even unappealing ("Can you stay late and help me put this proposal together?").

Skills at asking for help are as vital to success as skills at providing it. It makes a difference if the request is clear, the reason for the request is evident, and the time frame explicit. And it matters whether the request is conveyed with the affect of a slavedriver or that of a respectful colleague.

When we request the help of others, we had better be ready for a variety of responses.

My daughter Carolyn was recently married. It was a large and complex wedding with many unique, lovely touches. Carolyn and her fiancé Lee, in addition to their full-time jobs, assumed the role of "project managers" for the big event. Because they live hundreds of miles from the wedding site, they had to depend upon the good will—and help—of many friends and family members.

Thus began several months of remotely arranging the litany of necessities so well known to brides and grooms and the families of brides and grooms: tents, gowns, flowers, the cleaning of the Old

Meetinghouse, the rehearsal dinner, the reception dinner, and scores of other details. Many times the couple found themselves saying, "I need your help."

Carolyn reported that responses to their requests for help fell into four categories, each of which had a profoundly different impact on bride, groom, and wedding. All who have spent time in the workplace will have no difficulty recognizing them.

1. REFUSAL

"I'm sorry, I'm just too busy right now to go shopping for gifts for the bridesmaids with you."

At work one might hear, "I'm sorry, working on a proposal for that client just doesn't fit in with my other priorities right now."

When one asks for help, of course, one places him- or herself in a vulnerable position, risking being an imposition or being rejected. It's perilous either way. Fortunately, preparation for a wedding brings out a generosity of spirit not always present in the workplace. Carolyn and Lee seldom had to deal with the anger, disappointment, and guilt that accompany asking for help and being rejected.

2. REDEFINE

"Why do you want poached salmon for the reception? Don't you really want a side of beef? I know someone who can dig you an open pit barbecue!"

At work one might hear, "What you really need to propose is a 20 percent discount which means you'll have to have accounting redo the numbers." A common response to our request for help is one in which helpers redefine the situation, and therefore the assistance that will be needed from them. Unfortunately, for anyone trying to "check off" items from a long list of what is needed—and needed fast—a redefinition of the situation is not helpful. Indeed, it is usually infuriating.

3. YES . . . THEN

Often we request help and our colleague promises to comply. We think the matter is now "handled." Then four days later a phone call comes: "I've found the doilies you wanted in a catalog, but they can't promise delivery in time for the wedding." Or, an e-mail three days later announces, "I've found a store that has fourteen but not twenty, will that do?"

Or, at work: "I redid your numbers and think that you need to consider these four additional expense categories."

In effect, rather than being divested of the problem, we have now been introduced to yet additional problems. We feel not relief but exasperation. "It would be easier to do it myself," we have all said at one time or another.

4. "I'VE GOT IT COVERED"

Music to our ears!

The only wanted, needed, and welcome response to a request for help is, of course, "Yup, I've got it covered. Not to worry." A confident statement of assurance that the request will be honored. Then perhaps, when the issue has been addressed, one, and only one, confirmation that demands nothing more. For instance an e-mail that announces, "Here's the final seating arrangement you wanted." "Here's the cost analysis you need for your proposal."

Mission accomplished. No further entangling details. Item checked off!

These vignettes contain for all of us, whether under the wedding tent or in the office, a helpful **Working Rule 24**

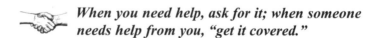 *When you need help, ask for it; when someone needs help from you, "get it covered."*

The likelihood we will get what we need from others is, of course, directly related to whether they have gotten what they needed from us. Reciprocal help is not only an indicator of a strong relationship; it is the stuff of which strong relationships are forged. How much we need, in our lives, to hear, "I've got it covered." How grateful we are. Whether we are trying to extricate ourselves in the middle of the night from a swarm of no-see-ums, planning a wedding, or writing a proposal, we can seldom make our way or attain our goals by ourselves. We depend upon family, friends, and colleagues and must ask assistance from them.

Just as to succeed, our family, friends and colleagues need to hear from us, "Got it covered."

Epilogue

So there you have it.

Just as education is what's left after you've forgotten everything you've been taught, so these *Lessons Learned* are "what's left" for me, my education from forty years at sea and in the workplace.

"A person who publishes a book willfully appears before the populace with his pants down. If it is a good book, nothing can hurt him. If it is a bad book, nothing can help him." I think Edna St. Vincent Millay said it all. I leave to you, dear reader, who has navigated these pages, the verdict.

As I ponder the foregoing stories, idiosyncratic though they may be, I am struck by their wide applicability. Who knows? If these cruising and working rules were broadly adopted, what a wonderfully bonding, balming, and civilizing effect they might have on the workplace, legislatures, international affairs, on the crime rate in our society—and on marriages, children, and families. What a wonderful world it would be!

But let's face it: all relationships are tough. These rules have become indispensable for me not only in weathering relationships but also in protecting and enriching them. Try them. Refine them. Embellish them with the wisdom from your own experience.

Best of all, honor, disclose, and celebrate your own lessons learned. For each relationship offers and deserves its unique set of lessons. If these stories from me succeed in unlocking stories from you, my effort will have been a success.

It might well be said of a lasting, robust relationship what the late oceanographer Jacques Cousteau said of the sea: "once it casts its spell it holds one in its net of wonder forever."

Cruising Rules Glossary

Adrift: State of locomotion undesirable for a sailboat.

Aground: Where you go if you don't consult the chart, and where, once gone, you never reveal you have been.

Anchor: Piece of ship's equipment designed to sink.

Ashore: Where those who would rather be sailing are.

Buoy: That part of a mooring designed to float.

Captain: He who is always right.

Cat's-ass brindle: The most beautiful hue in the world.

Chart: What you consult so you won't go aground.

Comfort Factor: That which is to be considered if you want to enjoy sailing.

Command: What the captain gives.

Crew: They who obey.

Cruise: Two or more days spent continuously on a boat that is underway, with stops for the night.

Cruising Rules: What one must comply with aboard ship to avert interpersonal capsize.

Davy Jones: Keeper of every ship's locker.

Dinghy: (a) Small boat with multiple uses, which may be towed behind a larger vessel if properly secured on a cleat. (b) Container for landing fish—and fisherman.

Down East: Where people end up, who head Up North.

Esso Map: What you consult if you wish to go aground.

Fatal Attraction: Irresistible urge on the part of ship's equipment to transfer residence from above to below sea level.

Feeling: Unfamiliar equipment members of the male species have but don't know how to use.

Florida: Liquid state in which the sailing water remains all year long.

Head: (a) What you use when you employ the Comfort Factor. (b) What you employ for comfort.

Laughter: That which enables a relationship to continue.

Mooring: Heavy block of granite, underwater, encrusted with prescription sunglasses, to which many a vessel is sometimes secured and by which it may sometimes be sunk.

Motor: That which every proper sailing vessel must have but never use.

Paint: What the boatyard does.

The Ratio: A number that exists but must never be calculated.

Relationship: State of tenuous connection between people, continuously at risk when on a sailing vessel.

Return: What a sailor must never promise to do.

Sailing: Where I'd rather be.

Sink: (a) Stainless compartment into which valuables such as cameras and binoculars may safely be stowed. (b) What a boat does when responding to a total Fatal Attraction.

Story: Form of discourse (along with joke and lie) in which it is acceptable to engage while aboard ship.

Town Fathers: The mariner's Greek Chorus.

Trouble: That which you should be sure you're in before swimming nude across a harbor.

Truth: That which the captain speaks.

Winch Handle: Essential, metallic, elbowlike appliance usually found (or lost) in mud at ocean's bottom.

Wind: (a) Air that passes a sailing vessel propelling it, usually (but not always), forward. (b) Air that passes within a sailing vessel propelling others, usually, away.

Zucchini: Most essential and ubiquitous piece of terrestrial cargo taken to sea.

Cruising Rules

Cruising Rules are the norms of personal behavior required for individuals to stay on speaking, even friendly, terms while confined together for an indefinite period in close quarters at sea.

Cruising Rule 1 *page 2*

Any story worth telling is worth telling often.

Cruising Rule 2 *page 4*

When a party is talking, he is not to be interrupted until he has completed everything he wants to say.

Cruising Rule 3 *page 7*

A statement, joke, or story offered with the intent of humor shall be responded to with audible, visible, persistent, and, above all, authentic laughter.

Cruising Rule 4 *page 10*

Any statement made as fact is, in fact, true and is therefore to be accepted as the truth.

Cruising Rule 5 *page 14*

Whoever you show up as for a cruise is who you are, and you are to be received accordingly.

Cruising Rule 6 *page 18*

Nondiscussibles may be discussed only within swimming distance of home port.

Cruising Rule 7 *page 22*

The hand that holds the paintbrush determines the color.

Cruising Rule 8 *page 26*

That which secures us may also sink us.

Cruising Rule 9 *page 29*

Whatever is cooked by someone else is to be received, savored, and celebrated with the words "Good though!"

Cruising Rule 10 *page 33*

The gods protect beginning sailors and fools—sometimes both at once.

Cruising Rule 11 *page 38*

Any damage incurred by a vessel is due to a deficiency in the equipment and not to the judgment or competence of the individual involved.

Cruising Rule 12 *page 42*

Reef early and often.

Cruising Rule 13 *page 47*

> *Loose lips sink egos.*

Cruising Rule 14 *page 51*

> *The rightful resting place for every piece of equipment on board is at the bottom of the sea.*

Cruising Rule 15 *page 57*

> *Be careful who you get into a boat with.*

Cruising Rule 16 *page 61*

> *Too many captains spoil the brine.*

Cruising Rule 17 *page 67*

> *Before you go to great lengths to extricate yourself from trouble, make sure you're in trouble.*

Cruising Rule 18 *page 72*

> *When you cruise alone, be prepared to navigate the "inside passage."*

Cruising Rule 19 *page 76*

> *Ships can pass in the day—as well as the night!*

Cruising Rule 20 *page 81*

> *If you have to ask how much it costs, you'll never be able to enjoy it.*

Cruising Rule 21 *page 85*

> *Never let anyone on board who has to get off board—for God's sake!*

Cruising Rule 22 *page 89*

When you go to sea, don't promise to return—especially at an agreed-upon time.

Cruising Rule 23 *page 96*

When you declare your intention to sail in a particular direction, the winds will come strong from that direction.

Cruising Rule 24 *page 103*

When in the thick of it, go through the thin of it.

Working Rules

W orking Rules are the norms of personal and professional behavior required for individuals in the workplace to stay on friendly terms and, in addition, produce a distinguished product.

Working Rule 1 *page 3*

Every story—and every storyteller—has value.

Working Rule 2 *page 5*

Pay attention!

Working Rule 3 *page 8*

Laugh with others often, audibly, and visibly.

Working Rule 4 *page 11*

Others know what they are talking about—unless proven otherwise.

Working Rule 5 *page 16*

Bring your real self in and accept and celebrate colleagues who bring their real selves in.

Working Rule 6 *page 19*

When nondiscussibles are discussed, progress will be made.

Working Rule 7 *page 23*

If you want to have your say, you've got to be present for the conversation.

Working Rule 8 *page 27*

Our strengths may become our weaknesses.

Working Rule 9 *page 31*

Acknowledge and applaud not only accomplishment but also effort.

Working Rule 10 *page 36*

Mistakes rarely become problems unless compounded by more mistakes.

Working Rule 11 *page 39*

There is no reward in punishment.

Working Rule 12 *page 44*

Keep your balance—or fall.

Working Rule 13 *page 48*

Loose lips float ships.

Working Rule 14 *page 54*

Be careful what you work for.

Working Rule 15 *page 59*

To perform like a team, act like a team—together.

Working Rule 16 *page 63*

> *There can never be too many leaders . . . or followers.*

Working Rule 17 *page 68*

> *Finding your place—or places—may take a lifetime.*

Working Rule 18 *page 73*

> *The most critical relationship is the one you have with yourself.*

Working Rule 19 *page 79*

> *Planning is hard; execution is harder.*

Working Rule 20 *page 83*

> *If you have to ask how much it costs, you may never value it.*

Working Rule 21 *page 86*

> *To achieve excellence one must want to become good enough bad enough.*

Working Rule 22 *page 93*

> *Underpromise and overdeliver.*

Working Rule 23 *page 100*

> *When moving forward, be sure to get out of your own way.*

Working Rule 24 *page 105*

> *When you need help, ask for it; when someone needs help from you, "get it covered."*

**CORWIN
PRESS**

The Corwin Press logo—a raven striding across an open book—represents the happy union of courage and learning. We are a professional-level publisher of books and journals for K-12 educators, and we are committed to creating and providing resources that embody these qualities. Corwin's motto is "Success for All Learners."